005.4

Jim Gate.

D0493912

BERNARD BABANI (publishing) LTD
The Grampians
Shepherds Bush Road
London W6 7NF
England

www.babanibooks.com

Please Note

Although every care has been taken with the production of this book to ensure that all information is correct at the time of writing and that any projects, designs, modifications and/or programs, etc., contained herewith, operate in a correct and safe manner and also that any components specified are normally available in Great Britain, the Publishers and Author do not accept responsibility in any way for the failure (including fault in design) of any project, design, modification or program to work correctly or to cause damage to any equipment that it may be connected to or used in conjunction with, or in respect of any other damage or injury that may be so caused, nor do the Publishers accept responsibility in any way for the failure to obtain specified components.

Notice is also given that if equipment that is still under warranty is modified in any way or used or connected with home-built equipment then that warranty may be void.

First Published – April 2015

British Library Cataloguing in Publication Data:

A catalogue record for this book is available from the British Library

ISBN 978-0-85934-754-9

Cover Design by Gregor Arthur

Printed and bound in Great Britain for Bernard Babani (publishing) Ltd

About this Book

Android 5 Lollipop continues Google's tradition of using confectionery names for versions of its Android operating system, such as Lollipop and its forerunner Android 4.4 KitKat.

Android 5 Lollipop introduces many new features which have been highly praised. You can buy new devices such as the Nexus 6 smartphone and the Nexus 9 tablet with Lollipop pre-installed. Or you can upgrade to Lollipop from an earlier version of Android, such as KitKat, using a free, easy to install update.

This book is intended to help new users of tablets and smartphones to quickly get started with Lollipop. Users of earlier versions of Android can use this book to learn how to upgrade their device to Lollipop and then enjoy the new features. These include the Material Design interface, improved notifications and security and the new Overview carousel showing running apps.

Earlier chapters explain the main features of the Lollipop OS and the necessary hardware and useful accessories, such as Chromecast for mirroring your device onto a TV screen. Setting up a new user account and connecting to Wi-Fi is also explained.

The Google Play Store has millions of apps, many of them free, and Chapter 3 shows how these can be downloaded and managed on your device. The Library for all your eBooks, music and videos, as well as the Calendar, Google Maps and using your device as a Sat Nav are then described.

Entertainment such as live and catch up TV, music and video are discussed as well as communicating using Facebook, Twitter, Gmail, Skype and Google Hangouts. Browsing the Internet using Google Search and Google Voice Search is then covered.

The use of the on-board cameras to take photos, as well as importing photos from other sources such as SD cards and flash drives are described. Transferring and sharing photos and other files using Dropbox and Google Drive, as well as Bluetooth and Near Field Communication (NFC) are also covered.

About the Author

Jim Gatenby trained as a Chartered Mechanical Engineer and initially worked at Rolls-Royce Ltd., using computers in the analysis of jet engine performance. He obtained a Master of Philosophy degree in Mathematical Education by research at Loughborough University of Technology and taught mathematics and computing for many years to students of all ages and abilities, in school and in adult education.

The author has written over forty books in the fields of educational computing, Microsoft Windows and more recently, tablet computers. His most recent books have included "An Introduction to the Nexus 7", "Android Tablets Explained For All Ages" and "An Introduction to the hudl 2" all of which have been very well-received.

Trademarks

Google, Google Drive, Google Chrome, Chromecast, Gmail, Google Cloud Print, Hangouts and YouTube are trademarks or registered trademarks of Google, Inc. Microsoft Windows, Microsoft Word, Microsoft Publisher, Microsoft Excel and Skype are trademarks or registered trademarks of Microsoft Corporation. Facebook is a registered trademark of Facebook, Inc. Twitter is a registered trademark of Twitter, Inc. Amazon Kindle is a trademark or registered trademark of Amazon.com, Inc. Dropbox is a trademark or registered trademark of Dropbox, Inc. All other brand and product names used in this book are recognized as trademarks or registered trademarks, of their respective companies.

Acknowledgements

I would like to thank my wife Jill for her support during the preparation of this book and also Michael Babani for making the project possible.

Contents

3

Exploring the Lollipop OS   27

4

Further Features   41

7

Browsing the Web 81

8

Communication and Social Networking 91

Photos and the Clouds 103

Essential Jargon

App

An application or program which a user runs, such as a game.

Operating System (O.S.)

The software used to control all aspects of the running of a computer. *Android 5 Lollipop* is Google's latest Android O.S.

Processor

A chip executing millions of program instructions per second.

RAM (Random Access Memory)

The main memory, temporarily storing the current app.

Internal Storage

Permanent storage used to store apps and data. Usually in the form of an SSD (Solid State Drive) with no moving parts.

Cloud Computing

Saving files on large *server computers* on the Internet, leaving more space on the Internal Storage of your tablet computer.

Syncing

Automatically copying and updating your files to the clouds, i.e. the Internet, so they are accessible to other computers.

Online

Connected to the Internet.

Screen Resolution

The number of dots or *pixels* on the screen, such as 1920x1080 (HTC One (M8)), or 2048x1536 (Nexus 9).

Streaming

This allows you to watch videos or listen to music *temporarily*, without saving a copy on your tablet's Internal Storage.

Downloading

A file is copied from the Internet and saved on your tablet. It can be accessed anytime in the future, even if you are offline.

Android 5 Lollipop: An Overview

What is the Android Operating System?

In the world of tablets and smartphones, Android is the name given to the most popular *touchscreen operating system* or *OS* for short. (A typical Android icon is shown on the right). An operating system is a suite of programs which control the basic functions of any computer, including tablets and smartphones. The main functions are:

- Starting up and shutting down the smartphone or tablet.
- Connecting the device to the Internet.
- Providing the user interface, screens, icons and menus.
- Managing the memory.
- Running the user's current programs or *apps*.
- Managing peripheral devices such as printers.
- Saving data files on the Internal Storage of the computer.
- Uploading and storing files in the *Clouds*, i.e. the Internet.

The main operating systems used on tablets and smartphones are Android and iOS. Android is used on a large range of devices from different manufacturers whereas iOS is just used on Apple iPads and iPhones. As discussed later in this book, you can use a laptop or desktop computer to manage the files on the Internal Storage of an Android device.

The Operating System vs Apps

The Operating System

The Android operating system is built into a tablet or smartphone from new and is running whenever the computer is switched on. All computers are controlled by programs, i.e. sets of instructions written in a special language or code. As discussed on the previous page, the operating system is a suite of programs used to control the basic functions of a computer and is known as *system software*.

What is an App?

In earlier times, programs written to perform tasks such as payroll calculations on large mainframe computers were known as *applications software*. Nowadays programs which the user chooses to run for a particular purpose are known more briefly as *apps*, especially on hand-held devices.

Apps must be written for a particular operating system. So an app written for Android tablets and smartphones will not be compatible with a version written for Apple iOS devices. However, an app written for Android 5 Lollipop should be compatible with all of the various devices which use Lollipop.

When you buy a new Android device a lot of icons are already installed, such as the icons for the Google apps shown below.

Google   Gmail   Chrome   Photos   Earth

In addition there are over a million apps for Android devices in the Google Play Store. These can be downloaded and installed on your tablet or smartphone. Later on, apps from the Play Store which you no longer require can be deleted from your device.

The Evolution of the Android OS

Android was developed from an earlier operating system called *Linux*, which is used in a wide variety of computer types. Linux and Android are known as *open-source* operating systems, meaning that manufacturers can modify them to suit their own devices. This has made Android popular with a wide range of manufacturers of smartphones and tablet computers. However, most devices use the same common core of standard or *stock* Android features.

Unlike the operating systems used on laptop and desktop computers, Android uses touchscreen finger *gestures* involving *tapping*, *swiping*, *holding* and *sliding* objects on the screen.

Android has been developed by Google, Inc., famous for the well-known Google search program and also for mapping the world with Google Earth and Google Street View. The Lollipop OS includes *voice search* and *speech recognition*.

Although Android is used in Google's own Nexus smartphones and tablets, many other manufacturers also install Android in their devices. These include well-known manufacturers of tablets and smartphones such as Samsung, Sony, Asus, LG and HTC. Since Google is primarily a software company, it uses other companies to manufacture its tablets and smartphones, such as Motorola (Nexus 6), Asus (Nexus 7) and HTC (Nexus 9). These companies also produce their own Android devices.

Although the rival Apple smartphones and tablets are probably the most popular from a single company, they are outsold by the total number of Android devices from many different manufacturers.

Versions of Android are named after confectionery, such as Ice Cream Sandwich (version 4.0), Jelly Bean, (4.1, 4.2, 4.3) and KitKat (4.4). Android 5.0 Lollipop was launched in November 2014 and at the time of writing in 2015 there have already been updates 5.0.1 and 5.0.2.

Android 5 Lollipop

As mentioned earlier, the Android OS is used on more smartphones and tablets than any other OS. Android 5 Lollipop introduces a number of major changes which should make Android even more popular. Some of the new or improved features included in Android 5 Lollipop are listed below.

- A new user interface, called Material Design, with redesigned screens and icons which are brighter and more colourful. Lollipop works faster and smoother than previous Android versions.

- A new feature allowing *multiple users* of the device — not previously available on smartphones, only on tablets.

- Improved notifications which pop-up when new messages arrive or appointments are imminent. Notifications also appear on the Lock Screen. Tap to open the notification.

- Control over which notifications are displayed and when.

- Double tap the screen to wake from sleep mode.

- Battery saving mode to extend battery life.

- A new **Overview** or multi-tasking button which displays previous screens as cards in a revolving carousel.

- **Google Now** cards on the left of the Home screen.

- A single **Gmail** app which also manages e-mails from other services such as Hotmail and Yahoo!

- Improved **Messenger** texting feature.

- **Pinning** feature to keep children, for example, in an app, preventing access to other apps.

Some of these new features are illustrated on the next page. All of the new features are described in more detail in the rest of this book.

Some New Features in Android 5 Lollipop

Material Design interface: smoother, more colourful

Previous screens appear as cards in a revolving carousel

Google Now cards now part of the Home screen

Single e-mail app handles Gmail, Hotmail, Yahoo!, etc.

Notifications now appear on the Lock or startup screen

A smartphone can now have multiple users, previously only available on tablets

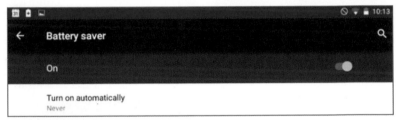

Battery saver mode switches off non-essential background functions when the battery is low

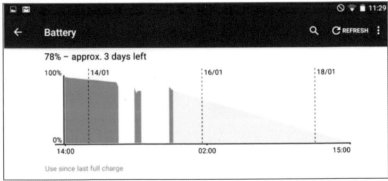

Remaining battery life and usage is monitored and displayed

The Google Play Store

The fact that there are over a million apps in the Play Store, many of them free, means that Android tablets can be used for a vast range of activities. Apps in the Play Store produced by third party companies are checked by Google so they should be free from viruses or other problems. For security, the default settings of Android 5 Lollipop do not allow the installation of apps from sources other than the Play Store.

When you open the Play Store by tapping its icon shown on the right, the following menu bar is displayed.

Tap **APPS** shown above and then tap **CATEGORIES** to see the vast range of subjects for which there are apps available.

A small sample of the categories is shown on the right. There are apps to cover seemingly every conceivable activity such as **Health & Fitness**, **Finance**, **Music & Video**, **News & Magazines**, **Photography**, **Travel**, **Sports** and **Shopping**, etc.

Categories
Games
Books & Reference
Business
Comics
Communication

Favourite apps which I have downloaded include the following:

Amazon Kindle   BBC iPlayer   Cat Sounds   Flightradar 24

Some Popular Apps

Apps appear as icons on the Home screen and the All Apps screen, as discussed in more detail in Chapter 3. An app is launched using a single tap on its icon, using a finger or a stylus. Listed below are some very popular and useful Android 5 Lollipop apps, together with their icons.

Play Store

The **Play Store** icon gives access to over a million apps in different categories. These are either free or can be bought online for a few pounds. When a new app is installed on your computer its icon appears on the Home and All Apps screens.

Google

Google is a famous *search engine*. "To Google" means to search for information on a particular subject, after typing in some relevant *keywords.* Lollipop also includes *voice search* for entering the keywords by speaking.

Chrome

Google Chrome is a *web browser*, similar to Microsoft's Internet Explorer and Apple's Safari. A web browser is used to display web pages and to move between pages using *links*. You can also revisit web pages from your *browsing history* or which you've *bookmarked* for future viewing.

Gmail

Google mail or **Gmail** is a free and popular e-mail service allowing you to send and receive messages consisting of text, pictures and attached files. Creating a Gmail account and password gives you access to several other Google services.

Earth

Google Earth allows you to zoom in and view different parts of the globe, using satellite images, aerial photography and images taken by cameras mounted on cars all over the world.

YouTube

YouTube is a free Google website which allows individuals and companies to upload and share videos for other people to view. These may include amusing incidents or popular music videos. If a video spreads quickly and is viewed by millions of people, it is said to "go viral".

Skype

Skype allows you to make free Internet telephone calls between computers. The Skype app is free and Android devices generally have the necessary built-in microphone, speakers and cameras. These enable free *video calls*, as well as voice calls, to be made to friends and family all over the world.

Facebook

Facebook is the leading *social networking* website. Users of Facebook post their *Profile* or *Timeline* on the Internet, allowing them to become online *friends* with people of similar interests. Friends exchange news, information, photographs and videos, etc. Businesses and celebrities can also use Facebook for publicity.

Twitter

Twitter is another very popular social networking website, on which users post short messages or *tweets* (up to 140 characters long). Some celebrities use Twitter to air their views and they may have thousands of followers. You can follow whoever you like, send replies to *tweets*, or use Twitter to enlist support for a campaign.

Amazon Kindle

Android devices have their own app, Google Books, for reading eBooks, but you can also download the free **Kindle** app, the software used on the original Kindle eBook reader from Amazon. There are millions of books, magazines and games available to download cheaply.

Typical Uses of Android 5 Lollipop

With so many apps in the Play Store, the versatility of an Android device is phenomenal, as illustrated by the typical uses below.

- Reading the latest news and weather forecasts.
- Reading online editions of newspapers and magazines.
- Reading eBooks using Google Books or the Kindle app.
- Listening to music and watching videos.
- Watching live and catchup TV and radio.
- Importing, viewing and editing photographs.
- Searching the Web for information using the Google search app and the Google Chrome web browser.
- Searching the Web using *Google Voice Search*.
- Using Google Maps and Google Earth.
- Using an Android device as a Sat Nav.
- Sending and receiving e-mails.
- Using social networks, such as Facebook and Twitter.
- Using the *Skype* Internet telephone service to make free, worldwide, voice and video calls.
- Shopping online for goods, flights and holidays, etc.
- Tracking the delivery progress of items ordered online.
- Playing games such as Solitaire and Chess.
- Finding the answer to obscure crossword clues.
- Creating and editing text documents and small spreadsheets, including *speech recognition* text input.
- Tracking live flight information of aircraft including location, speeds, altitude, bearing and ETA.
- Managing your online bank account and finances, making payments and transferring money.

Interacting with a Touch Screen Device

The main methods are:

- Tapping icons on the touch screen or tapping characters on the on-screen keyboard, using a finger or a *stylus*.

- *Voice recognition* using spoken search criteria or spoken text input e.g. for e-mail or word processing.

- External keyboards are available which may also act as a protective cover. Accessories such as alternative keyboards, etc., are discussed on page 14.

Touch Screen Gestures

- A single *tap* on an icon opens an app on the screen.

- Tap where you want to enter text and the *on-screen keyboard* pops up ready for you to start typing.

- *Swipe* a finger across the screen quickly without hesitating, e.g., to scroll across the Home screen. Swiping can also unlock a locked screen and open the Quick Settings window. (Swipe down *twice* from the top).

- *Touch and hold* an item such as an app or a widget, before *sliding* slowly to a new position with the finger.

- *Double tap* to zoom in or zoom out of a screen. In some apps *pinching* two fingers together or *stretching* apart can be used to zoom out or zoom in. This is useful, for example, to enlarge a web page in Google Chrome or make an area easier to see in the Google Maps app.

The Menu Icon

The 3-dot menu icon shown on the right appears on many screens (in various colours). Tap this icon to see a list of options relevant to your current activity.

The On-Screen Keyboard

The touch screen method of controlling the computer works very well in most situations. The on-screen keyboard, shown below, pops up whenever you tap in a slot intended for the entry of text.

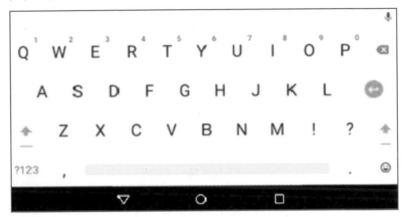

The icons on the *Navigation Bar* along the bottom of the on-screen keyboard above have the following functions:

Hide the on-screen keyboard.

Return to the Home screen, discussed in Chapter 3.

Display recently visited pages in the form of a revolving carousel, as shown on page 28.

The Stylus

If you find accurate typing difficult using the on-screen keyboard, a cheap *stylus*, (around £2 or less) as shown on the right, may help. The stylus has a soft rubber tip to prevent damaging the screen.

Entering Text Using Voice Recognition

When entering text in an app such as Google Docs, as mentioned in Chapter 9, the on-screen keyboard displays a microphone icon, as shown on the right and below. (You may need to tap the blank text area to display the icon when using Gmail, for example).

Tap the microphone icon to open the voice recognition window, ready for you to start speaking the text into the word processor or e-mail app, etc.

The Google Voice Search

As discussed later, when searching with Google, instead of typing the keywords for the search, tap the microphone icon as shown on the right and below.

This opens a window displaying the words **Speak now** and the icon shown on the right. Then speak the search keywords, such as "Charles Dickens", for example. The device responds with a list of links to web pages giving information about the great writer.

Using a Separate Keyboard

If you want to use a tablet or smartphone like a laptop, you can buy a separate keyboard, as shown on the right. These include the Google Nexus 9 Keyboard Folio and various alternatives.

Some keyboards double up as a case and may be held in place magnetically. *Bluetooth* is used to connect the keyboard to the Lollipop device. As discussed on page 110, Bluetooth is a technology for connecting devices wirelessly over short distances.

The OTG (On The Go) Cable

This is an extremely useful accessory. The small connector on the right is inserted into the *Micro USB port* on the device, shown on page 18. The large socket shown on the OTG cable is a standard *USB port* which can

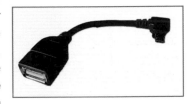

be used to connect the following devices to the device.

- Digital camera for viewing and transferring photos.
- SD card reader for extra storage and transferring files.
- USB *flash drive* or *memory stick* for transferring files.
- USB keyboard and mouse, connected using USB cables.
- USB dongle for a wireless keyboard and mouse.

Pages 106 and 107 give more details of accessories which can be connected to Lollipop devices. These include alternative keyboards, card readers and flash drives, etc.

2

Getting Set Up

Introduction

There are two ways you can equip yourself to start using the Android 5 Lollipop operating system:

- Buy a new tablet or smartphone with Lollipop pre-installed.

Or:

- Upgrade an existing device which has an earlier version of Android installed, such as Android 4 KitKat.

Upgrading an Existing Device

Upgrading an existing Android smartphone or tablet to Lollipop is achieved using a free *OTA* (*Over The Air*) *update*. If your device is capable of being upgraded and your manufacturer has decided to adopt the Lollipop OS, you will receive a notification on the **Settings** page on your tablet or smartphone. This is discussed in detail on pages 19 and 20.

New Devices with Lollipop Pre-Installed

Android 5 Lollipop was launched by Google in November 2014, in conjunction with the new Nexus 6 smartphone and the Nexus 9 tablet. At the time of writing it's expected that other major companies such as Sony and HTC will pre-install Lollipop from new on their devices in 2015. Shown on the next page are the technical specifications of two leading devices which run Android 5 Lollipop. Apart from the screen size, the smartphone and the tablet are very similar in many respects. Large smartphones like the Nexus 6 are also known as *phablets*.

Typical Lollipop Device Specifications

Shown below are some specifications for the flagship Nexus 9 tablet and the HTC One (M8) smartphone. At the time of writing, the upgrade to Android 5 Lollipop for the HTC One (M8) is being rolled out worldwide

	Nexus 9	HTC One (M8)
Device Type	Tablet	Smartphone
Android O.S. version	5 Lollipop	5 Lollipop
Processor speed	1.7GHz	2.3GHz
Internal storage	16 or 32GB	16 or 32GB
Memory (RAM)	2GB	2GB
Screen resolution (pixels)	2048x1536	1920x1080
Screen size (diagonal)	8.9 inches	5.0 inches
Cameras	Front 1.6MP Rear 8MP	Front 5MP Rear 4MP
Battery life (approximate)	9 hrs 30mins	10 –14hrs

(Some of the above terms are explained in **Essential Jargon**, opposite page 1).

The table above shows that, in some respects, the HTC One (M8) smartphone is more than a match for the Nexus 9 tablet. Both devices compare well with many laptop and desktop computers in terms of computing power, (such as processor speed and memory or RAM) .

The HTC One (M8) smartphone above also has a *microSD* card slot, providing additional storage of up to 128GB.

Some tablets and smartphones also have an *HDMI* port allowing the Android 5 Lollipop screen to be displayed on a TV screen via an HDMI cable.

Preparing to Use a New Device

When you first take a Lollipop tablet or smartphone out of the box, you may be surprised that such a small device can actually be a powerful computer. This is possible because, unlike a laptop or desktop computer, the tablet or smartphone doesn't need the bulky components like a hard drive, power supply unit, CD or DVD drive or large sockets to accommodate cables for peripheral devices. Thanks to advances such as *cloud computing*, based on the Internet, these large components, normally found in laptop and desktop computers, are not needed in Lollipop devices.

Charging the Battery

Apart from the tablet or smartphone itself, the only other contents in the box are usually the battery charger plug and cable and perhaps a couple of flimsy leaflets. No assembly work is needed. Although the battery may be partially charged on delivery, you are advised to charge it fully before you get started. One end of the charging cable plugs into the *micro USB port* on the bottom of the tablet or smartphone, as shown on the next page. The other end of the cable has a full-size USB connector which can be inserted into the 3-pin 13-amp charger plug provided. Alternatively the charging cable can be inserted into a USB port on a laptop or desktop computer. Charging using a computer should be carried out with the Android 5 Lollipop device in sleep mode or switched off. This method of charging is slower than when the Android is connected to a charger plugged into a wall socket.

As described elsewhere in this book, Android 5 Lollipop introduces a new **Battery saver** feature for extending battery life. Lollipop also monitors and displays details of battery usage.

The battery life between charges is often quoted as approximately 9-10 hours, depending on the type of activity.

Front Camera Speaker Headset socket Rear Camera

Microphone

Power/Lock key

Volume key

Speaker Micro USB port Microphone

The illustration above shows the main features of the Nexus 9 tablet, which has Android 5 Lollipop installed from new. Other tablets and smartphones have similar features although the layout on individual devices may be different.

As discussed earlier, some devices have a microSD card slot, providing extra storage up to 128GB and simplifying transferring files such as photos from a camera, etc. This is also helpful for storing your files such as music and video collections which can then be used offline, perhaps when you're away from W-Fi on holiday, for example.

The Free Lollipop Update

If you're using an earlier version of the Android OS, such as 4.4 KitKat or 4.1 Jelly Bean, you'll probably be able to replace it with Lollipop using an *OTA* (*Over The Air*) update. This is a process which started in November 2014 and involves the downloading of the Lollipop OS over the Internet to your device. Google devices like the Nexus 5, 7 and 10 were the first to receive updates to Lollipop. Updates are also underway now, or planned in 2015 for other Android tablets and smartphones, from companies such as Asus, Samsung, Sony, Motorola, LG and HTC. The availability of the update is controlled by each manufacturer and also depends on your location in the world.

You can check the availability of the update as follows. Swipe your finger down from the top right of the screen and tap the **Settings** icon, shown on the right, on the **Quick Settings** panel. This opens the main **Settings** screen. Scroll up and tap **About tablet** at the bottom of the 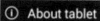 main **Settings** screen. Next tap **System updates** at the top left of the **About tablet** screen, as shown below.

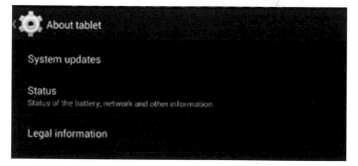

If the Lollipop update is available for your device, the notification shown at the top of the next page should be displayed. At the time of writing Android 5.0.2 Lollipop was the current update.

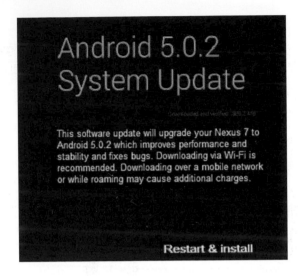

The notification above was received on my Nexus 7 after checking the **System updates,** as described on the previous page. Tap **Restart & install** shown above to begin the updating process. You're informed of progress and after about ten minutes the update to Android 5 Lollipop should be finished.

Although the screen colours and layout are different in Lollipop, you can still open the **About tablet** page as described on page 19. However, you now swipe down _twice_ to open the **Quick Settings** screen. As shown below, the **About tablet** page now displays **Android version 5.0.2,** i.e. the latest version of Lollipop at the time of writing.

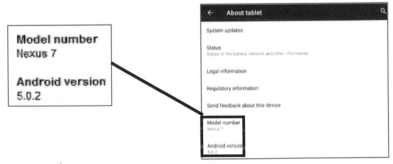

Starting Up

Hold down the *Power/lock key*, shown on the top right in the example on page 18, until the word **Google** appears on the screen, followed by the *Lock* screen as shown below. Next *swipe* the padlock icon across the screen to open the *Home* screen, discussed in the next chapter.

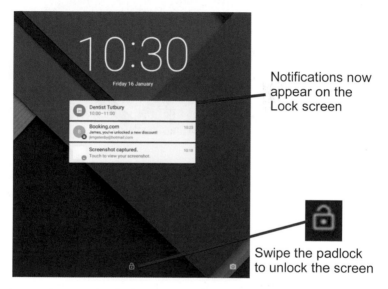

Notifications now appear on the Lock screen

Swipe the padlock to unlock the screen

Various other methods for unlocking the screen, such as setting a *PIN number* or a *password*, are discussed in Chapter 5.

The screenshot above shows that *Notifications* now appear on the Lock screen as well as the Home and All Apps screens. These include, for example, appointments from your calendar, files you've downloaded and e-mails received. Double tap a Notification on the Lock screen to display the Notification in full.

Shutting Down

It's best to shut down the device properly at the end of a session. Hold down the Power/Lock key shown on page 18 and then tap **Power off** in the small window which appears after a short time.

Connecting to Wi-Fi

In the home, this often means connecting to a **broadband router**, usually included when you take out a contract with an Internet Service Provider such as BT, Virgin or Sky. Or it may mean connecting to the Wi-Fi network in a hotel or café, etc.

After selecting your language, the tablet or smartphone should automatically detect any available Wi-Fi networks. Alternatively swipe down _twice_ from the top of the screen to display the **Quick Settings** panel shown below.

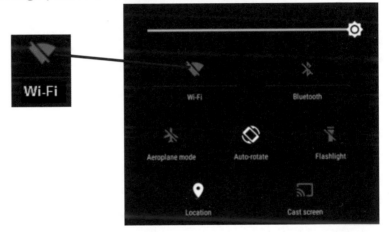

Now tap **Wi-Fi** or its icon shown above. If necessary, on the next screen to appear, tap the circle shown on the right and below to turn **Wi-Fi On**. This displays a list of available networks in your locality, as shown below.

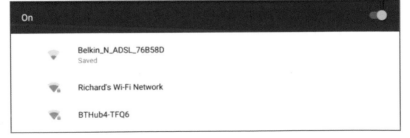

The small padlock icon shown on the right indicates a *secure network,* requiring a password to be entered before you can connect to it.

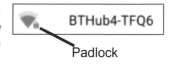

Padlock

Tap the name of the router or network you wish to connect to. The on-screen keyboard, shown on page 12, automatically pops up, enabling you to enter the password for the network, as shown below.

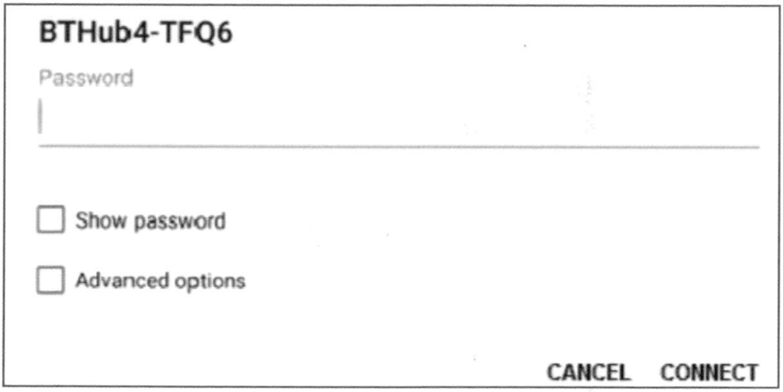

BTHub4-TFQ6

Password

☐ Show password

☐ Advanced options

CANCEL   CONNECT

The name and password for a home network can usually be found on the back of the router. In an establishment such as a hotel or café, you may need to ask the staff for the password for their Wi-Fi. Some organisations now provide free Wi-Fi and you may not need a password.

Tap **CONNECT** shown above to complete the process of getting online to the Internet. The word **Connected** should now appear next to the name of your selected router or Wi-Fi network, as shown below.

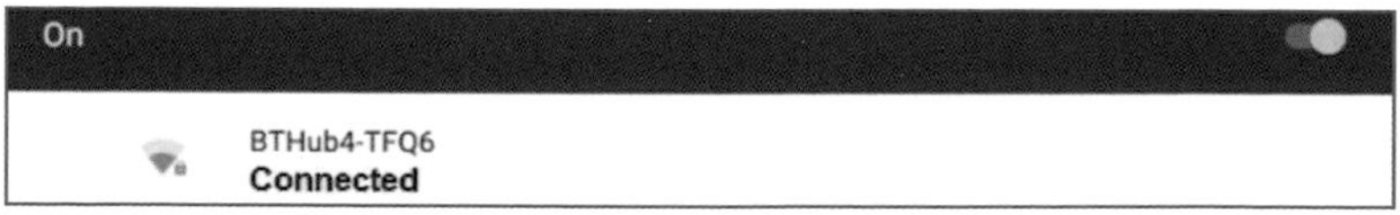

On

BTHub4-TFQ6
Connected

Checking Your Wi-Fi Connection

You can check your Wi-Fi settings at any time by swiping down _twice_ from the top of the screen to display the **Quick Settings** panel shown on page 22. Instead of "**Wi-Fi**", the panel should now display the name of your network, such as **BTHub4-TFQ6** as shown on the right. The amount of white in  the sector shown on the right and above indicates the strength of the Wi-Fi signal. Tapping the sector switches the Wi-Fi On and Off.

If you tap the name of your network, such as **BTHub4-TFQ6** in this example, the list of all of the nearby networks is displayed, as shown at the bottom of page 22. The word **Connected** should appear next to your network as shown at the bottom of page 23.

Tap your network's name in the list of available networks to see the **Status** of your connection, as well as the **Signal strength**, **Frequency**, type of **Security**, etc., as shown below.

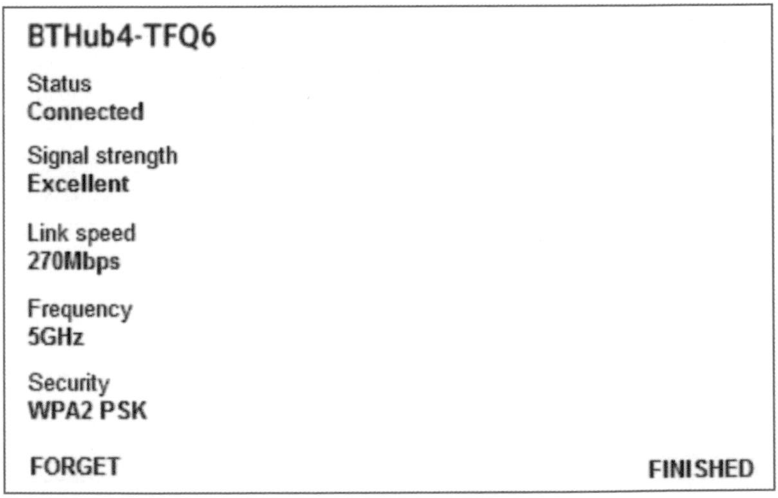

BTHub4-TFQ6

Status
Connected

Signal strength
Excellent

Link speed
270Mbps

Frequency
5GHz

Security
WPA2 PSK

FORGET   FINISHED

Tap **FORGET** shown above to remove a redundant network from the list, such as a network you used while on holiday.

Creating a Gmail Account

If you haven't got a Gmail account with an e-mail address and password, you can create one during the initial setting up process for a new device. It's worth opening a Gmail account because it gives access to several other free Google services, such as Google Drive cloud computing, as discussed in Chapter 9. Drive includes the Google Docs free office software.

You can create a new Google account at any time after swiping down twice from the top of the screen to open the **Quick Settings** panel. Then tap the **Settings** icon at the top of the panel, as shown on the right and below.

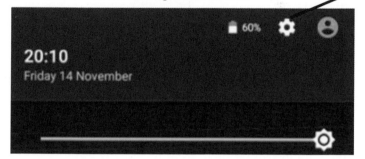

Another **Settings** icon, shown on the right, appears on the All Apps screen discussed in Chapter 3. Tapping either of the **Settings** icons opens the main **Settings** screen shown on page 58. Tap **Accounts** and then tap **+ Add account**. Then tap **Google** and **CREATE A NEW ACCOUNT**. Then enter your name and a suitable e-mail address and password, such as **jimsmith@gmail.com**. If the e-mail address has already been taken, add a few numbers to make it unique, such as **jimsmith99@gmail.com**.

Sharing Google Drive and Google Docs with a PC or Mac

With a Google account you can access Google Drive and Google Docs on your Android device and also on PC and Mac computers at **www.google.com**.

Rotation of the Screen

Swipe down twice from the top of the screen to open the **Quick Settings** panel shown on page 22. Tapping the icon in the centre of the panel changes the display between the **Portrait** and **Auto-rotate** modes shown on the right.

In **Portrait** mode, the display is fixed for viewing with the tablet in the upright position, i.e. with the long sides vertical. In the **Auto-rotate** setting, when you turn the device through 90 degrees, the screen display also rotates so that you can still read it.

Sleep Mode

If you don't use the tablet or smartphone for a set period of time while it's switched on, the screen goes blank. This is the low power consumption *sleep mode*. You can also put the device into sleep mode by briefly pressing the Power/Lock button shown on page 18.

Sleep mode saves battery life and may also be necessary for security if you leave the tablet or smartphone unattended. When you wake the device up from sleep mode, you need to unlock it by swiping the padlock icon discussed on page 21 or using one of the other *unlocking* methods discussed in Chapter 5.

Waking Up from Sleep Mode

> Tap the screen twice
>
> Or: Press the Power/Lock key

Setting the Inactivity Time Before Sleep Mode is Entered

Tap the **Settings** icon shown on page 25 and select **Display** from the main **Settings** screen shown on page 58. Then tap **Sleep** and tap to select the required period of time from the list, which has options from 15 seconds to 20 minutes.

3

Exploring the Lollipop OS

The Home Screen

When you start the smartphone or tablet by holding down the Power/Lock key and unlocking the screen, as discussed on page 21, the *Home screen* opens as shown on the right. The Android 5 Lollipop operating system introduces new screen colours and wallpaper patterns known as *Material Design*.

There are several panels on the Home screen, viewable by sliding or swiping horizontally in either direction.

To launch an *app* or program, tap its icon on the Home screen. A lot of apps are already installed on a new tablet or smartphone and you can add more from the Google Play Store. Icons for your favourite apps can be placed on a personal Home screen for convenience.

The Navigation Bar at the bottom of every screen, is shown below. The left-hand icon opens the previous screen while the middle one opens the Home screen. The right-hand *Overview* icon opens a revolving carousel display of "cards" showing previously opened apps, as discussed on the next page.

The Overview or Multitasking Feature

This shows your previous apps like cards arranged in a carousel. To start the display, tap the **Overview** button, shown on the right, on the Navigation Bar at the bottom of all the screens, as shown on the previous page.

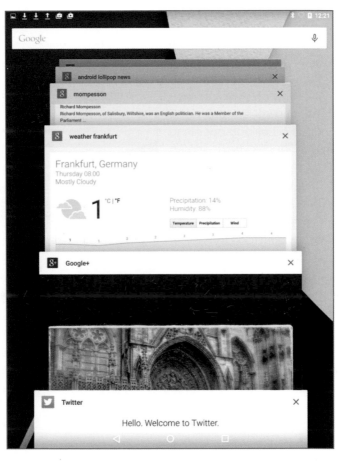

To change the cards in the foreground, gently swipe upwards or downwards. To open a particular app, tap anywhere on the card. To close an app, tap the cross in the top right-hand corner.

The Favorites Tray

Along the bottom of the Home screen is the *Favorites* tray shown below, giving quick access to frequently used apps.

The icons on the Favorites tray above are as follows:

 Google Mail is an extremely popular e-mail service, discussed in more detail later in this book.

 The **Google Chrome** web browser is used to display and navigate web pages.

 This icon displays the **All Apps** screen shown on the next page.

 Tap this to watch popular **YouTube** online videos.

 The **Photos** app stores and manages all your albums, photos and videos, as discussed in Chapter 9.

 This launches either one of the two cameras on the device, as discussed in detail in Chapter 9.

The **All Apps** icon above is a fixture on the Favorites tray — the others can all be replaced with apps of your own choice.

The All Apps Screen

When you tap the All Apps icon on the Favorites tray, shown on the right, an All Apps screen like the one below appears, displaying up to 30 apps. In fact you can have several All Apps screens as you add more apps from the Play Store, as discussed later in this chapter. Frequently used apps can be copied from the All Apps screens to make up a personal Home screen of your favourite apps.

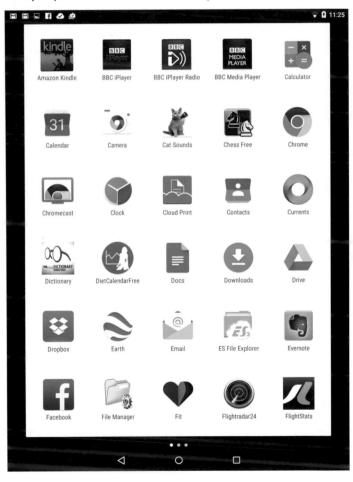

Customising the Favorites Tray

The default Favorites tray is shown below. The All Apps icon shown on the right and below is fixed on the Favorites tray. The other icons can be moved or deleted and replaced on the Favorites tray with apps of your own choice.

Removing an App from the Favorites Tray

Touch and hold the icon for the app you want to remove from the Favorites tray. Hold your finger on the icon until **X Remove** appears at the top of the screen. Without lifting your finger, drag the icon over **X Remove** and drop it, deleting the app or folder. Please note that removing an app from the Favorites tray doesn't uninstall the app from the device. Its icon still appears on the All Apps screen. Alternatively, move an app from the Favorites tray and slide it onto another part of the Home screen.

Moving an App to the Favorites Tray

Clear a space on the Favorites tray by moving or removing an icon, as described above. To move an app on the Home screen to the Favorites tray, hold your finger over the icon, then drag the icon to the space on the Favorites tray. In the example below, the **Maps** icon has been added on the left. (You can have up to six apps of your own on the Favorites tray).

The red **YouTube** icon shown on the right and above has been removed and replaced by a circular *folder* icon shown on the lower right. This folder includes the **Facebook** app. Folders are discussed on the next page.

Putting Apps in Folders

The circular icon shown on the right represents a *folder*, containing several apps. Folders can be created on the Home screen and also placed on the Favorites tray. For example, you might want to create a folder for all your games or all your music apps. Or you could put the  apps for **Facebook**, **Twitter** and **Skype**, shown below on the Home screen, in a folder called **Social**, for example.

On the Home screen, touch and drag the icons, one on top of the other, to form a single circular folder icon shown on the left below. Tap the folder icon to reveal the contents and to give a name to the folder. As shown below, tap **Unnamed Folder** and enter a name of your choice, such as **Social** in this example.

Tap a circular folder icon to view the apps within, as shown in the middle below. Then tap an icon to launch one of the apps.

Customising Your Home Screen

You can tailor your Home screen in the following ways:

- Change the background colour or wallpaper.
- Delete any apps and widgets you don't want.
- Copy from the All Apps screen any apps that you use regularly and place them on a personal Home screen.

Your personal Home screen can show just your most frequently used apps, in addition to those on the Favorites tray. To organise your apps further, you can group them in folders, as discussed on the previous page.

(The apps placed on the Home screen are only *copies*, so removing them from the Home screen doesn't remove them from the All Apps screen or uninstall them completely.)

Changing the Wallpaper on Your Home Screen

Hold your finger on an empty part of the Home screen until the following icons appear.

Tap the **WALLPAPERS** icon shown above then select a design from the samples at the bottom of the screen, as shown below. Tap **Pick image** on the left below to use a photo of your own.

Tap **Set wallpaper** at the top left of the screen to apply the new wallpaper, i.e. background, to the Home screen.

Deleting Apps from the Home Screen

You can safely remove redundant apps from the Home screen. Tap and hold the unwanted app until **X Remove** appears at the top of the screen. Then drag the app over **X Remove**. As the apps on the Home screen are only *copies*, they are still available on the All Apps screen.

Unlike the Home screen, care should be taken with the All Apps screen, where it's possible to *uninstall* apps completely. If the uninstalled apps are needed in the future, they will need to be reinstalled from the *Play Store*, as discussed shortly.

Adding Apps to Your Home Screen

To make up a personal Home screen with the apps you find most useful, open the Home screen where you want the apps to appear. Clear the screen of any apps and widgets you don't want. This is done by touching and holding the app or widget, then dragging onto **X Remove**, as described previously.

Tap the All Apps icon as shown on the right then touch and hold the app you want to move to the Home screen. The Home screen opens. Keeping your finger on the app, slide it into the required position on the Home screen. Part of a personal Home screen is shown below.

Widgets

A *widget* is an icon which is used to display information such as a calendar, your most recent e-mails, the weather or a clock, as shown on the right. Widgets appear alongside of apps on the Home screen, as shown on page 27. Tapping a widget displays more information, such as the weather forecast, on the full screen.

Viewing the Installed Widgets

Tap and hold an empty part of the Home screen until the **WIDGETS** icon appears, as shown in the centre below.

Tap the **WIDGETS** icon shown in the middle above to see the widgets already installed on your tablet or smartphone, such as the **Bookmarks** and **Calendar** widgets shown below.

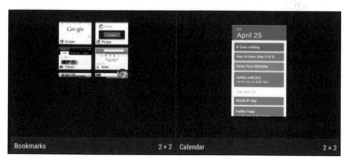

Tap and hold a widget to add it to your Home screen. You can install more widgets from the Play Store, (after tapping **APPS/CATEGORIES/Widgets**) in the same way as apps, as described on the next page.

Getting Apps from the Play Store

Apps and widgets pre-installed on a new device can be supplemented by apps downloaded from the Play Store, either free or costing a few pounds. To open the Play Store, tap its icon shown on the right, on the All Apps screen or on the Home screen.

The Play Store

The Play Store has over a million of apps and widgets arranged in groups such as games, movies (to rent or buy), music, books and magazines (**NEWSSTAND**), as shown below.

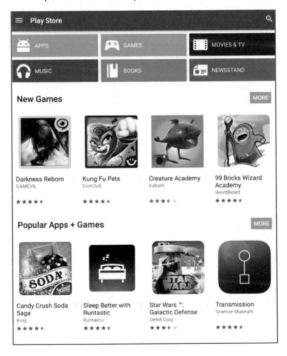

Scroll through the various **Categories** to find a particular app. Alternatively, you can carry out a search for an item such as an app, game, movie or book, etc., as discussed on the next page.

Searching the Play Store for Apps

As an example, a search will be made for an app to enable a device to be used as a music keyboard.

First tap **APPS**, as shown on the main Play Store screen shown on the previous page. Then tap the magnifying glass search icon, as shown on the right.

Typing the Keywords

The search bar appears as shown below, with a flashing cursor ready for you to type the name of the app or widget you wish to search for. The on-screen keyboard pops up automatically. Enter the keywords for the search, such as **music keyboard** and tap the search key (magnifying glass icon) on the keyboard.

The Voice Search

Tap the microphone icon shown on the right. The small window shown below appears, requiring you to speak the keywords, such as **music keyboard**.

The Android 5 Lollipop speech recognition system is most impressive and immediately finds lots of music keyboard apps, as shown on the next page. You might like to practise searching for a few apps using the microphone. Apps I found in this way included **chess game**, **route planner** and **sound recorder**.

Downloading and Installing Apps

The search for music keyboards results in a long list of apps, as shown in the sample below. Most of these are free.

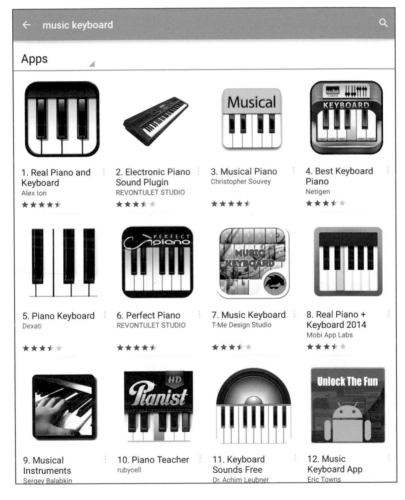

To obtain an app, first tap its icon as shown above. If it's free, the word **INSTALL** appears on the right. If there is a charge, the price is shown on the right, instead of **INSTALL**.

For a free app, tap **INSTALL** to download the app to your device. An icon for the app is placed on your All Apps screen and on your Home screen. The app should now be ready to use.

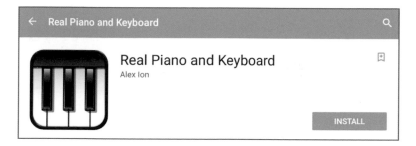

If there is a charge for an app, tap the price and you will then need to buy it by providing your bank details, before proceeding to install it as before.

Deleting Apps from the All Apps Screen

After touching and holding an app you previously installed, the word **Uninstall** appears at the top of the screen, next to a dustbin icon, as shown below.

If you slide the app over the dustbin icon or **Uninstall**, the app will be removed from the device. If you need the app again you will need to reinstall it from the Play Store.

Default Apps or widgets are those already installed on the All Apps screens when the tablet or smartphone was purchased. These default apps and widgets do not have the **Uninstall** option when you touch and hold their icons in the All Apps screen. Only the words **App info** appear at the top of the screen, allowing you to view details about the app and also there is an option to **DISABLE** the app.

Key Points: Apps and Widgets

- The Android 5 Lollipiop device is "driven" by tapping icons representing apps and widgets.

- Apps are small applications or programs such as a web browser, a game or a drawing program.

- Widgets are small windows, usually displaying information such as a calendar, news or an e-mail inbox.

- The All Apps screen shows all of the apps installed on the device.

- The Home screen consists of several panels which can be customized to display selected apps and widgets.

- Apps and widgets can be copied to the Home screen by touching and holding, then sliding onto the Home screen.

- Further apps and widgets can be downloaded from the Google Play Store. New apps are placed on the All Apps screen and the Home screen automatically.

- At the bottom of every Home screen is a Favorites tray which displays 6 icons for frequently used apps.

- The user can change 6 of the apps on the Favorites tray.

- The Favorites tray also displays the All Apps icon.

- Widgets cannot be placed on the Favorites tray.

- Related apps can be grouped together and placed in folders, such as Painting, Photography, Games, etc.

- Folder icons are circular, can have a name and can be placed on the Favorites tray.

- Apps on the Home screen are only copies. Deleting them doesn't remove them from the All Apps screen.

- The Navigation Bar at the bottom of all the screens has icons to open the Home screen, to display the last screen visited and show recently used apps in rotating windows.

Further Features

Introduction

This chapter looks at some more of the features built into the Android 5 Lollipop operating system. The features described in this chapter are:

Google Now and Google Cards

This feature provides Google searching for information using both voice and text queries. Google Cards automatically displays useful, real-time information for your current location.

My Library

This is a widget that displays all the books, movies, music, etc., that are already on your tablet or smartphone.

Calendar

Keeps track of all your appointments and sends reminders of imminent events, synchronised to your various devices.

Google Maps

Displays maps of anywhere in the world, including Satellite View and Google Earth.

Sat Nav

The built-in Global Positioning System together with Google Maps enables an Android 5 Lollipop tablet or smartphone to be used as a *Sat Nav*.

Google Now

This is an extension to the popular Google search engine. Google Now employs GPS (Global Positioning System) satellite technology to pinpoint your exact, current location. This is used to gather local information such as the weather and traffic conditions.

Google Now doesn't require any setting up. You just need to make sure **Location** is switched on in the **Settings** and **Mode** is set to **High accuracy** as discussed on pages 47 and 48.

To open Google Now, swipe up from the bottom of the screen, or tap the Google icon on the All Apps screen, shown on the right. You can also open Google Now by swiping right from the Home screen. The Google Now screen opens with a search bar across the top, as shown below.

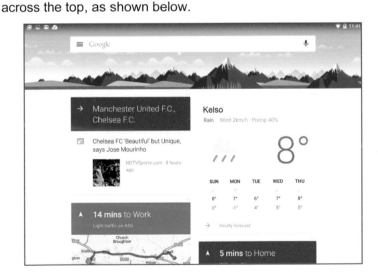

As shown above, Google Now displays a series of panels known as *Google cards*, relating to your current location or recent searches with Google.

Searching in Google Now

Typing Keywords

The search bar in Google Now shown below allows you to enter the keywords for a search, such as **weather in Florence** for example, by typing using the on-screen keyboard.

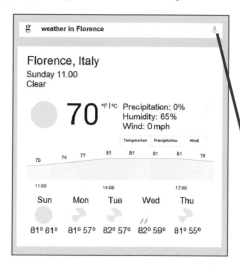

Spoken Queries

You can also tap the microphone icon, as shown above and on the right. Then speak your query into the device. Using spoken queries is discussed in more detail on page 37. The results of the search may produce a spoken answer, as well as a Google Card, as shown above. You will also see some traditional Google results as shown below, which you can tap to open web pages relevant to your search.

Weather in Florence, Italy | 14 day weather outlook of Florence
www.worldweatheronline.com/Florence-weather/Toscana/IT.aspx
Latest **weather in Florence** Weather, Italy. Florence 14 day weather forecast, historical weather, weather map and Florence holiday weather forecast.
Weather Map - Florence, Italy weather - Monthly Averages

Perhaps you could experiment with a few spoken queries. For example, I said "tabby cat" with the microphone selected and received a spoken answer and a list of traditional Google search results with links to web pages, as shown below.

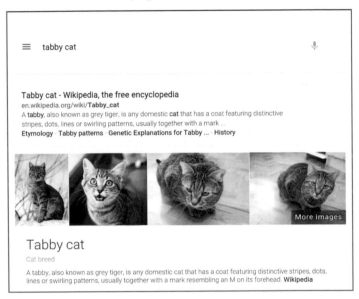

Sporting Fixtures

If you enter or speak the name of a favourite sports team, such as Chelsea FC or Manchester United, Google Now gives the latest result and details of their next fixture.

Google Search Icons

The two icons for searching shown below are used regularly in Lollipop. You can also launch a voice search from the Home screen by saying "Ok Google" .

Google Search   Google Voice Search

More on Google Cards

Google Cards pop up on the Google Now screen without you taking any action. For example, suppose you enquire about flights at your local airport, or about traffic on local roads. Google Now responds with Google Cards based on your recent activities. Google Cards are continually updated automatically, giving reminders of imminent events from you Calendar, fixtures for your favourite teams and news on topics you've been researching. You may also receive weather news based on your current location identified by the device's built-in *GPS* (*Global Positioning System* based on information from satellites).

After you swipe up from the bottom of the screen, Google Now display cards based on your previous activities and interests, such as the football results and share prices shown below.

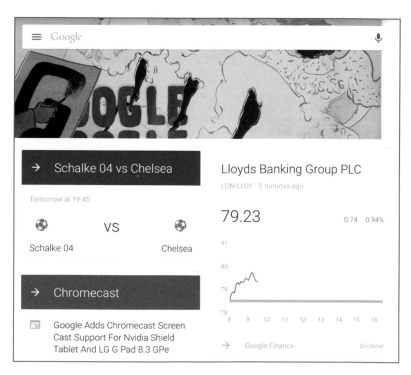

The Google Now Menu

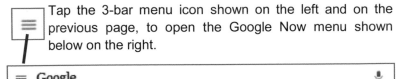

Tap the 3-bar menu icon shown on the left and on the previous page, to open the Google Now menu shown below on the right.

Reminders can be created to pop up on Google Now when a particular event is imminent.

Customise allows you to select topics for which you wish to receive updates in Google Now, under the headings **Sports**, **Stocks**, **Places**, **TV & video**, etc.

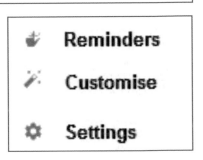

Settings above opens a sub-menu for Google Search and Google Cards. This allows you to switch Google Now Off and set various search and other options. (Switching Google Now On is discussed on the next page).

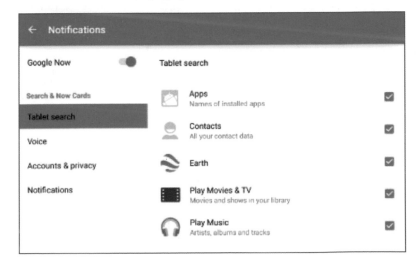

Making Sure Google Now is On

In order to use Google Now to display cards as shown on page 45, a number of features need to be switched on. These are probably already switched on by default, but you can easily check, as shown below. The main settings needed to fully use Google Now are:

- Google Now: **ON**
- Location: **ON**
- Location Mode: **High accuracy**

If Google Now is Off, when you swipe up from the bottom, or tap the Google icon on the Home screen, you only see the basic Google screen, not the more colourful Google Now screen, as shown on page 45.

Switching Google Now On

Swipe up from the bottom of the screen. If Google Now is Off, the words **GET GOOGLE NOW** appear in a box across the screen. Tap this box and the **Get Google Now** screen appears, as shown below. Tap **YES, I'M IN**, as shown at the bottom right below to turn Google Now On.

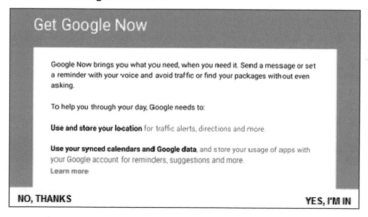

Switching Location (GPS, etc.) On

Swipe down twice from the top of the screen to display the **Quick Settings** panel shown on page 56. You should see the **Location** icon in white, if **Location** is switched On.

To make sure **Location** is On, tap the **SETTINGS** icon as discussed on page 25 and then under **Personal** tap **Location**, as shown below.

The following screen opens, allowing you to make sure **Location** services are **On**, if necessary by tapping the circular button on the right.

Tap **Mode** shown above and from the window which opens as shown below, tap the button to select **High accuracy**. This makes sure that **GPS**, **Wi-Fi** and **mobile networks** are all used to identify your current location.

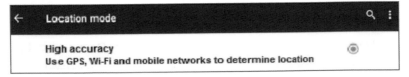

My Library

This is a widget that allows you to display all the music, magazines, books and movies that are installed on a device. Some of these media may be already installed from new or you may have added more from the Google Play Store.

The **My Library** widget may already be displayed on one of your Home screens. If not, open the **Widgets** screen as described on page 35 and scroll across until you see the **Play – My Library** widget as shown on the right. Touch and hold this widget, then slide it into a convenient place on the Home screen. The **Play-My Library** window opens as shown below on the right, to display icons giving access to all of your installed media, i.e., **My music**, **My books**, etc. Tap **My Library** shown on the right to place the **My Library** widget on the Home screen, as shown below.

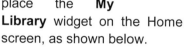

Tap any of the icons, **My music**, **My books**, **My newsstand**, or **My movies & TV**, to open your chosen medium.

To make room for **My Library**, widgets and apps which you no longer need can be deleted from the Home screen by holding and sliding over **X Remove** at the top of the screen.

The Calendar

The Lollipop Calendar includes the following features:

- Keeping a record of all your future events.
- Sending you notifications of imminent events.
- Synchronizing changes between various devices, such as your tablet, smartphone, laptop or desktop PC or Mac.

The Calendar is opened by tapping its icon, shown on the right, on the All Apps screen. The Calendar opens as shown at the bottom right below. A 3-dot menu button, shown on the right, at the top right of the calendar, opens the menu shown on the left below. This has options to display **Days**, **Weeks or Months**. **Schedule** lists your events in a list which can be scrolled vertically.

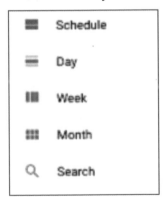

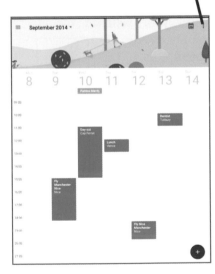

Scroll through the days, weeks or months by swiping horizontally.

Creating a New Event or Editing an Event

Tap the **New event** icon, shown on the right and at the bottom right of the calendar on the previous page. Now enter the details of the event such as the title, time and place.

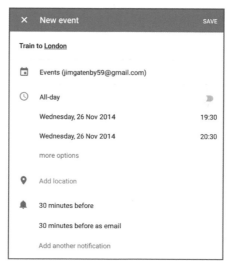

At the bottom of the **New event** screen you can set a reminder in the form of a notification or an e-mail. With a notification there is a beep and then an event, such as **Train to London** in this example, appears in the **Notifications** panel, as discussed on page 59. Tap the event name for further details.

To edit an existing event, double-tap the event's title on the Calendar, then tap the pencil icon which appears, as shown on the right. This opens the **Edit event** screen allowing you to amend the details.

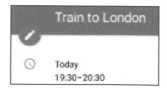

The Calendar Widget

A Calendar widget appears in the WIDGETS screen, as discussed on page 35. This can be copied to a suitable clear space on the Home screen. This is done by touching and holding the widget and then sliding it into position on the Home screen, as described in more detail on page 35. The Calendar widget lists all your forthcoming events, automatically updated with information from the Calendar app.

Calendar widget

Tap the Calendar widget to open the Calendar app full screen for editing existing entries or adding new events.

Syncing Your Calendar with a PC, etc.

The Google Calendar can be viewed on all the common platforms — tablet, smartphone, laptop or desktop PC or Mac, etc. On a PC or Mac open **www.google.co.uk**. If necessary **Sign in** with your Gmail address (or **Sign up** for a new one). Then select the **Apps** icon on the top right of the screen, shown here on the right. From the drop-down window which appears, select the **Calendar** icon, shown below, to open the Calendar.

New events can be added to the Calendar on any of your devices. Any changes to the Calendar are automatically synced across to all the devices you are signed in to with your Gmail address and password.

Google Maps

Lollipop has an icon for Google Maps already installed on the All Apps screen, as shown on the right. When you first tap the **Maps** icon, it opens to show a map of your current area. To find a map of another area, enter a *place name* or *post code* in

the search bar. In this example, **Farne Islands** was entered. Stretch or pinch the map with two fingers to zoom in or zoom out.

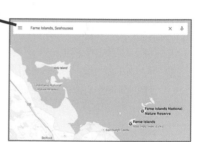

Tap the 3-bar menu icon, shown above, on the top left of the screen, to see a menu of alternative views of the area, i.e. **Satellite**, **Terrain** and **Google Earth**, as shown on the right below.

Terrain is the basic map view shown above on the right. Both **Satellite** and **Google Earth** display satellite images of the area. **Google Earth** has another menu, shown below on the left, allowing you to display additional information, such as businesses, places of interest, etc., as shown on the right below.

🖼	Satellite
🔺🔺	Terrain
🚫	Google Earth

Using Google Maps as a Sat Nav

The built-in *GPS* in Lollipop is used for identifying your precise location when planning a journey and also en route. Make sure **Location/GPS** is switched On, as shown on page 48. If your device is Wi-Fi only, set up a route *before* setting off, while still connected to the Internet. In Google maps, tap the 3-bar menu icon and select your mode of transport. Enter the

name or post code of your destination. Google Maps responds with the travelling time from your current location. Tap the time (e.g. **4hr 15 min** shown on the right). Traffic disruptions are listed, together with alternative routes which can be viewed by tapping the map shown below.

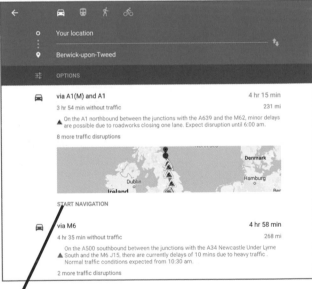

Tap **START NAVIGATION** shown above to start receiving spoken directions for each stage of your journey.

There are several other Sat Nav apps available in the Google Play Store discussed in Chapter 3, such as Navfree and CoPilot.

Settings and Security

Introduction

This chapter describes some of the most important and useful settings, in the Lollipop operating system.

The Quick Settings Panel

This allows you to see at a glance if some of the important features such as Wi-Fi and Bluetooth are switched on. Features can be switched on and off by tapping their icons.

The Settings Page

This page gives access to all the main settings such as Users, Apps, Battery, Display, Accounts and Security, etc.

Notifications

Messages which pop up to inform you of e-mails received, files downloaded, screenshots captured, calendar events, etc.

Locking the Device

A smartphone or tablet can be locked in various ways, using a password, pattern, PIN number or facial recognition.

Screen Pinning

When you lend someone your device, screen pinning locks them into a single app which you are happy for them to use.

NFC (Near Field Communication)

Copy data between devices by touching them back-to-back.

Backup and Reset

Make backup copies of your data and settings on Google's Web servers. The backups can be used to restore your data and settings on the device after a *factory reset* to solve a problem. The factory reset erases all of your data.

Quick Settings

Swipe down _twice_ from the top of the screen to display the **Quick Settings** panel shown below. (Alternatively swipe down once using _two fingers_ on the screen. Swiping down once with one finger displays the Notifications). The icons in the lower half of the panel are white when a function is switched On and greyed out with a line across them when the function is switched Off, as shown on the right and below. Tap an icon when you want to switch the function On or Off.

 This icon, at the top right of the **Quick Settings** panel above, gives the state of charge of the battery.

 Tap this icon, also shown at the top right above, to open the main Settings screen shown on page 58.

 New users can be added to a device after tapping the icon on the left and on the top right above. (Multiple users were not previously allowed on smartphones).

Beneath the time and date shown on the Quick Settings panel on the previous page is a brightness control, as shown below. To adjust the brightness, tap then slide the icon.

Icons on the Quick Settings Panel

**BTHub4-TFQ6
(Router)**

The icon shown on the left and on the Quick Settings panel on the previous page is used to display your router and to switch Wi-Fi On and Off, as discussed in Chapter 2.

Bluetooth

After tapping this icon you can switch **Bluetooth** On and Off. Pairing Bluetooth devices is discussed on page 110.

Aeroplane mode

Aeroplane mode switches the Internet Off for flight safety. Any eBooks, etc., to be read on a flight, need to be downloaded to the tablet or smartphone before boarding the plane.

Auto-rotate

The **Auto-rotate** button alternates between rotating the screen when the device is turned into landscape mode or keeping it fixed relative to the sides in portrait mode, as discussed on page 26.

Flashlight

The flash LED for the rear camera (if available) is switched On and Off using this icon.

Location

Location allows Google to determine your current location, as discussed on page 48.

Chromecast

This icon can be used to mirror the screen from a tablet or smartphone onto an HDMI TV screen, using the Google **Chromecast** dongle, as discussed on page 107.

The Main Settings Screen

As discussed on page 56, the **Settings** screen shown below can be launched by tapping its icon on the **Quick Settings** panel or the similar icon on the All Apps screen, as shown on the right.

Settings

Wireless & networks

▼ Wi-Fi   ✳ Bluetooth

○ Data usage   ⋯ More

Device

◐ Display   ♠ Sound & notification

▤ Storage   ▯ Battery

▊ Apps   ▲ Users

Personal

♀ Location   🔒 Security

▤ Accounts   ⊕ Language & input

☁ Backup & reset

System

◷ Date & time   ✝ Accessibility

Notifications

Swipe down from the top of any screen, including the Lock screen, to see your **Notifications**. These keep you up-to-date with, for example, your latest e-mails, calendar events, files received, devices connected and updates available, as shown below. Tap on a notification for more information or to take further action. Tap outside of the notifications to close the panel.

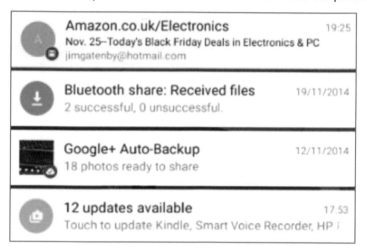

Notifications also appear as icons on the top left of the screen, as shown here on the right. In this sample, reading from the left, there are notifications of a screenshot captured, a video downloaded, a PDF file downloaded and a photo added.

The System Tray

This is a group of icons on the top right of the screen, as shown here on the right. In this example, reading from the left, there are icons showing Bluetooth On, Wi-Fi On and its connection strength, followed by the battery state of charge and the time.

Controlling Interruptions

You can control unwanted interruptions caused by notifications after selecting **Sound & notification**, as shown on page 58. Then use the sliders to set the **Media volume**, the **Alarm volume** and the **Notification volume** for your device.

Tap **Interruptions** to control what happens when interruptions arrive and to set priorities for different types of interrupt and times when interruptions are allowed, as shown below.

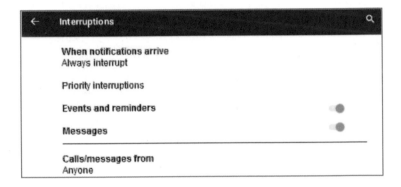

To control which apps can send notifications select **App notifications** from the **Sound & notification** page. Tapping an app such as **Calendar**, for example, lets you block or prioritise notifications from this app and also hide sensitive content.

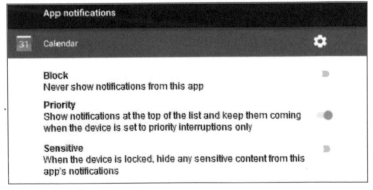

Security
Unlocking the Screen

When you first start up or "boot" Lollipop, the Lock screen is the first to appear, as shown on page 21. On a new installation of Lollipop, by default the Lock screen is opened by swiping an open padlock icon as shown on the right and on page 21. You also need to open the Lock screen after the device has been in sleep mode, as discussed on page 26.

If your tablet or smartphone contains sensitive information, there are several ways to prevent someone else from gaining access.

Open the main Settings screen from its icon on the Quick Settings panel or the similar icon shown on page 58, on the All Apps screen. Tap **Security**, as shown on page 58, then tap **Screen lock** from the **Security** page which opens.

As shown above, in addition to swiping the padlock icon, you can create a **Pattern** or set up a **PIN** number or a **Password**. In addition you can use *facial recognition*, as discussed on page 63, after first setting a Pattern, PIN or Password.

Creating a Pattern

Tap **Pattern** shown on the previous page, then use you finger to join up at least 4 dots.

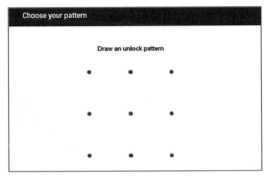

You need to draw the pattern again to confirm it. You can, if you wish, also choose to show Notifications when the screen is locked. Click **DONE** to complete the process.

Setting a PIN Number

Tap the **PIN** option shown on page 61. Enter and confirm your chosen PIN number.

As before you can choose to show Notifications on the Lock screen. Finally tap **DONE** to finish setting the PIN.

Setting a Password

Tap the **Password** option shown on page 61. The method of setting the password is very similar to setting a **PIN**, as described on the previous page.

Using Facial Recognition

This is an additional security measure which can only be implemented _after_ one of the other measures such as a pattern, PIN or password has been set up.

From the main **Security** page select **Smart Lock** near the middle of the page. Enter your pattern, PIN or password.

Now tap **Trusted face**, shown on the right, to switch facial recognition ON. After reading the precautionary notes about _face unlock_, tap **SETUP** at the bottom of the page. After tapping **NEXT**, position your face within a dotted line which pops up on the screen. Tap **NEXT** again and a tick should appear inside the facial area with the words **Got it** above, as shown below.

Now when you start the device the screen is initially locked with a _user_ icon as shown on the left instead of the padlock. Look at the screen and if your face is recognised the open padlock shown left above is displayed. This can be swiped to open the device. If your face is not recognised, swipe the closed padlock and enter your pattern, PIN or password to unlock the device. To test your security measures, you can press the Power/Lock key shown on page 18 to enter sleep mode, then press the key again to display the Lock screen. Now try to unlock the device.

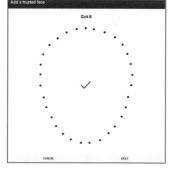

Setting Up Screen Pinning

From the main **Settings** screen shown on page 58, tap **Security**. Then scroll up and tap **Screen pinning** near the bottom of the Security page. Make sure **Screen pinning** is **On** as shown below, by, if necessary, tapping the green button on the right.

Open the app you want to pin. Now touch the **Overview** button shown below, on the Navigation Bar at the bottom of the screen.

Back  Overview

The **Overview** button displays your previous apps. A green and white pin icon, shown below on the left, appears on the last app you opened. Tap the pin icon to display the window shown below. To begin pinning tap **START**. **This locks the device into the last app opened**. To *unpin* the display, touch and hold the **Back** and **Overview** buttons, shown above, at the same time.

Pin icon

Use screen pinning?

Screen pinning locks the display in a single view.
To unpin, touch and hold Back and Overview at the same time.

☐ Ask for password before unpinning

NO, THANKS   START

Near Field Communication (NFC)

This is a new technology used to transfer data wirelessly between two NFC equipped devices. NFC can be used to pay for goods by tapping your device against a terminal in a store. Also to import data such as Web addresses and time-tables from *smart posters* and stickers known as *NFC tags*.

Many Android smartphones and tablets already have the necessary NFC chip built-in. You can use NFC **Touch and Go** to transfer the settings from an older device to a new one. NFC can also be used to copy photos, videos and Web pages, for example, between two NFC equipped devices.

Beaming a Photo Between Two Devices

Open the **Settings** page, as shown on page 58, and tap **More**, as shown below.

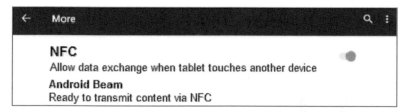

Make sure the devices are both unlocked and both have NFC on and the Android beam ready to transmit content, as shown above. Open the required photo (video or Web page, etc.) Bring the two devices back-to-back and move them about until you hear a distinctive sound. The screen will display **Touch to beam** and after tapping the screen, the photo will be beamed to the other device. Swipe down on the receiving machine and you should see the notification **Touch to view**, as shown below. The photo is saved in **Photos**, **On device** and in the **beam** section. Web pages and videos, etc., can be copied in a similar way.

Backup and Reset

This important feature appears on the lower left of the main **Settings** screen shown on page 58. Make sure both buttons are set to On as shown on the right below.

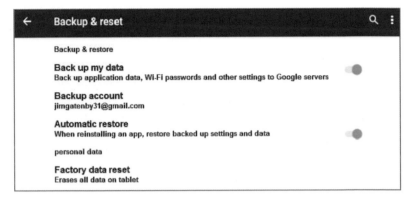

It's sometimes necessary to use **Factory data reset** to resolve problems with a smartphone or tablet. This wipes all your own data from the device. If you set the backup option and restore options as shown above, your data can be restored from the backup copies on Google's Web servers.

Factory data reset can be used to remove all your personal data before selling your tablet or smartphone to someone else.

Apps from Unknown Sources

Viruses can wreak havoc with a computer and its data. Some viruses are spread in software or apps. By default, Android devices can only run apps from the Play Store, which have been checked by Google. The **Unknown sources** option appears in the **Security** section of the **Settings** screen shown on page 58.

To be safe, make sure the **Unknown sources** option is switched Off as shown by the button in the left-hand position below.

Unknown sources
Allow installation of apps from sources other than the Play Store

Entertainment

Introduction

The following activities are discussed in this chapter:

- eBooks — electronic books which may be downloaded from the Internet for reading offline at any time.

- Music, magazines, movies and games downloaded for free or bought or rented.

- YouTube — a Google website which streams videos uploaded by the public and by commercial companies.

- Live and catchup TV and radio.

The small size and light weight of Lollipop tablets and smartphones mean you can use them literally anywhere — on a sofa, in bed or in a public place such as a restaurant. You can stow them in a bag and take them on holiday; many places such as hotels and restaurants now have free Wi-Fi so while you're away you can still go online for all your favourite Internet activities. The Lollipop device may also be used for your personal in-flight entertainment, if your airline allows it. *Aeroplane mode* or *flight mode* must be switched on to prevent possible interference with the aircraft's instruments. This was discussed on page 57 and only allows you to use the device *offline*, i.e. not connected to the Internet. Such offline activities would include reading an eBook or watching movies which have been saved for offline use, before boarding the aircraft.

eBooks

Many 20th century projects involved devices for reading books electronically on a screen. The Amazon Kindle, introduced in 2007, quickly became a best-seller, being extremely light and affordable and an efficient alternative to the printed book. Millions of eBooks are available to be downloaded from the Amazon Kindle Store and saved on a Lollipop tablet or smartphone, which can store far more books than most people are ever likely to read. (Figures in the thousands have been quoted, depending on what you take as the average size of an eBook).

- Android 5 Lollipop has its own app, *Play Books*, for reading eBooks and you can download books from the Google Play Store, which contains millions of titles.
- You can also install the free Kindle App and obtain books from the Amazon Kindle Store.

You can always delete any eBooks you no longer want, to save space on the internal storage of your smartphone or tablet

Google Play Books

When you first start to use Lollipop, there is already an icon for the Play Books app on the All Apps screen, shown on the right. If you read a lot of eBooks you may wish to copy the icon to the Favorites tray on the Home screen, as shown below. Changing the apps on the Favorites tray is discussed on page 31.

Play Books

Tap the Play Books app shown at the bottom of the previous page, then tap at the top left of the screen to display the menu shown on the right

Tap **My Library** to see all the books you've bought and to see samples recommended by Google.

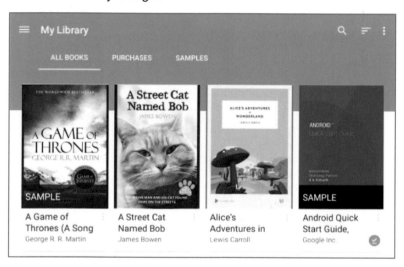

Tap **Shop** to open the Play Store as shown on the next page.

The Book section of the Play Store can also be opened by tapping the icon shown on the right, on the All Apps screen, then selecting **Books**, as shown below.

To search for a particular book, tap the magnifying glass icon shown on the right and at the top right of **My Library** shown above.

This opens the Play Store shown on the next page, displaying books which match your search criteria.

Books in the Play Store

In the Play Store you can browse through the various categories listed down the left, as shown below, check new arrivals and best selling books or look at the top free books.

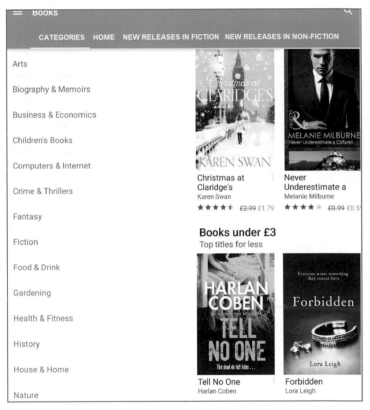

Alternatively you can search for a particular book after tapping the search icon shown on the right and above. Type the title of the book, replacing **Search Google Play** shown below. Or tap the microphone icon shown in the middle below and <u>speak</u> the title of the book.

For example, a search for **Bradshaws Guide** produced numerous results, as shown in the small sample below. Tap a book cover for more details or to buy the book. Alternatively tap the 3-dot menu button shown below, to the right of the book title, to add the book to a *wishlist* or to buy it. Some of the publications on this particular subject are free.

The 3-dot menu button on the lower right of a book cover is shown enlarged on the right. If the book's free, the option to add it to your library in the clouds appears, as well as the option to add it to your wishlist.

Add to library
Add to wishlist

If a book is not free, the option to buy the book is displayed. As shown on the right some books have an option to read some free *sample* pages.

Buy £4.91
Free sample
Add to wishlist

Once you've obtained a book, a small white tick on a blue shopping bag icon appears to the right of the title on the book's cover in the Play Store.

Once you've bought a book, you can read it from your Library in the clouds. Books in the clouds must be read when you're online. To read a book where there is no Wi-Fi, you need to download a copy of the book and save it in the internal storage of your phone or tablet. In My Library below, the right-hand book cover has a white tick in a blue circle, indicating that the book has been downloaded to the internal storage of the device.

Book can be read offline

Downloading a Book for Reading Offline

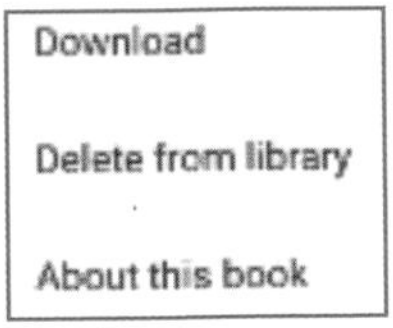

The book on the left above has no tick, as shown on the right-hand book. To make the book available offline, tap the cover of the book or tap the 3-dot menu button shown above and then tap **Download**.

Download

Delete from library

About this book

Deleting a Book

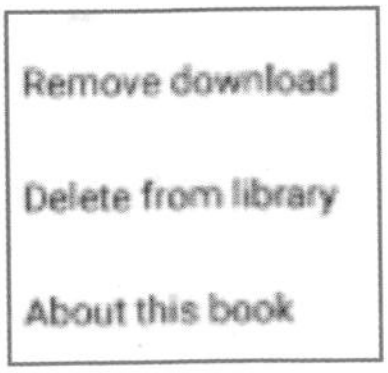

A book saved on the internal storage of the device can be removed after tapping the 3-dot menu button shown above and selecting **Remove download**. Tap **Delete from library** to remove the book from the clouds.

Remove download

Delete from library

About this book

Reading an eBook

Tap the Play Books app on the Favorites tray, or on the All Apps screen, to open My Library or Read Now, as discussed on page 69. Then tap the cover of the book you want to read. The book opens on the screen. Scroll backwards and forwards through the pages by swiping to the left

Play Books

or right, or tapping in the left and right margins. Tap anywhere on the text of the current page to view information about the page and to display various icons, etc., as shown in the top and bottom margins of the sample page below. Tap anywhere over the text again to switch off the icons and information.

Drag the blue ball on the slider shown below to advance rapidly forward or backward through the book.

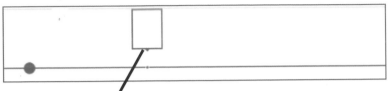

Tap the page thumbnail shown above to return to the page you were previously reading.

Across the top of the page, as shown above and on the previous page, the book title, author, chapter title and page number are displayed. The icons on the top right above have the following functions:

 Search for certain words and highlight them where they occur in the text.

 List chapter headings, page numbers and bookmarks.

 Change the brightness and formatting such as size of text, line spacing and font, etc.

 Open the menu shown on page 75, including options to add or remove a bookmark.

Bookmarks

Tap in the right-hand corner of the screen to add a bookmark in the top right-hand corner, as shown on the right. Tap a bookmark to remove it.

Using a Lollipop Device as a Talking Book

The Play Books app has a **Read Aloud** option. This feature can be used with many of the books and magazines in the Play Store. (As discussed on page 76, magazines can be obtained from the NEWSSTAND section of the Play Store).

To start reading aloud:

- Tap the cover of the book in My Library or Read Now.
- Tap anywhere on the text of a page to display the icons shown on page 74.
- Tap the 3-dot menu button also shown on page 74.
- From the menu which appears, tap **Read aloud**, as shown below on the right

The tablet or smartphone will now start reading the book aloud. To finish, tap over the text to display the 3-dot menu button and tap to display the menu shown on the right, but which now displays **Stop reading aloud**.

If you tap a book or magazine in My Library or Read Now, which is not compatible with this feature, the menu displays, in greyed out text, **Read aloud unavailable**.

Tapping **Settings** shown on the right opens a menu which includes options to use the volume key (shown on page 18) to turn pages and to use a "more natural voice."

Original pages

About this book

Share

Add bookmark

Read aloud

Settings

Help & feedback

Original pages shown in the above menu displays a *scanned image* of the original book in the *PDF* (Portable Document Format) file format. Normally eBooks are saved in the *ePub* file format, also known as *flowing text*. The **Original pages** option does not appear on the above menu on some books.

Reading Magazines

Open the Play Store after tapping its icon, as shown on the right, on the Home screen or the All Apps screen.

The Play Store has a **NEWSSTAND** feature, as shown below on the right and on page 36, where you can buy or subscribe to magazines in various categories. Some free magazines are also available.

Magazines are installed in a similar way to books, as just described. To start reading a magazine in your library, tap **MY LIBRARY** on the Home screen, then tap **My newsstand** shown on the right, as discussed on page 49.

Music in Lollipop

The methods used for obtaining and listening to music are very similar to those described earlier for books. Open the Play Store as described and tap **MUSIC** as shown above.

Then browse for the music you want, using the various **GENRES**, such as **Classical**, **Folk** or **Pop** and **TOP ALBUMS**, **NEW RELEASES** or **TOP SONGS**, etc.

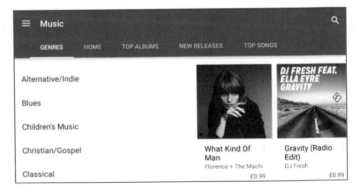

Google Play Movies & TV

The Play Store contains a range of movies and TV shows in various categories, etc., as shown below.

A movie may be bought or rented and you may have to begin watching a movie within 30 days of renting it and the rental may expire 48 hours after you start watching it.

To add a movie to a **Wishlist** for consideration later, tap the icon shown on the right and on the screenshot above. Alternatively tap **RENT** or **BUY** and after completing the transaction, the movie will be available in your Library. To watch the movie, tap the **Play Movies & TV** icon shown on the right, on the All Apps screen, then tap the movie graphic and tap the **Play** button.

Downloading a Movie for Viewing Offline

To make a movie watchable offline, tap the **Download** icon on the movie graphic, shown on the right. The circle starts to fill with red "ink" and when completely full the download is complete. The icon then displays a white tick in a red circle, as shown on the left and below. A *notification* of the download should also be displayed when you swipe down from the top of the screen, as discussed on page 59.

YouTube

YouTube is a website, owned by Google, which provides a platform for individuals, as well as commercial organisations, to share videos which they've made. These can rapidly "go viral" when millions of people watch them around the world.

To launch YouTube, tap the icon shown on the right. If the icon is not present on your smartphone or tablet, it can be downloaded from the Play Store and installed as described in Chapter 3. The YouTube screen shows a long list of video clips which can be scrolled up and down by swiping. Swipe from left to right to display the menu shown below.

To watch a video, tap a menu option such as **Popular on YouTube** or **Sport** and, if necessary, scroll vertically to display the cover picture and title of the required video. Tap the picture to start the video. To pause a video, tap the screen and then tap the pause button.

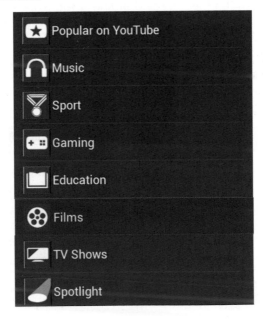

Live and Catch Up Television and Radio

The Google Play Store includes the free BBC iPlayer app, as shown on the right. This can be installed from the Play Store using the methods described in Chapter 3. Tap the icon shown on the right to open the BBC iPlayer as shown below.

BBC iPlayer

The row of icons on the upper right above enable you to search for and download programmes, switch between TV and radio and mark programmes as favourite. Tap the 3-dot menu button shown on the right and above to display the menu above on the right, which gives options to watch or listen to live TV and radio. Otherwise go back and watch or listen to programs broadcast previously, as shown below.

Games in the Play Store

The Google Play Store contains lots of free or inexpensive games in various categories, as shown below.

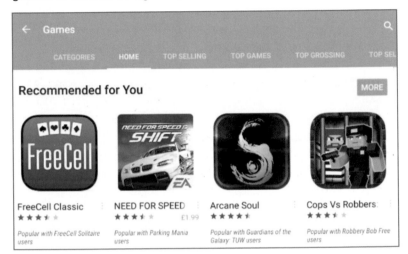

Games are installed as apps on your All Apps and Home screens, as discussed in Chapter 3. To launch a game, tap its icon, as shown on the right.

You may wish to group all of your games into one or more folders, as discussed on page 32 Tap the resulting circular folder icon to open the folder and give it a name. For quick access, the folder icon can be placed on the Favorites tray by sliding it into a gap created by sliding away another app, as discussed on page 31. In

the example below, the games folder has been placed on the extreme left of the Favorites tray.

Browsing the Web

Introduction

The Android 5 Lollipop smartphone or tablet gives you access to millions of web pages containing the latest high quality information on any subject you care to think of.

The *Google Chrome web browser* enables you to search the millions of web pages quickly and easily and displays the results in an attractive and readable format. Closely associated with Chrome, *Google Search* is the world's leading web search app on all platforms – tablet, laptop and desktop computers. An Android device, is an ideal tool for browsing the Internet using Google Chrome. In my opinion this rewarding and useful activity alone justifies the purchase of a smartphone or tablet, not to mention its many other functions such as voice and video messaging, news, social networking and entertainment, discussed elsewhere in this book.

Some of the main functions of Google Chrome are:

- To search for and display information after entering or speaking *keywords* into the Google search engine.

- To access web pages after entering their *address* such as **www.babanibooks.com** into the browser.

- To move between web pages by tapping *links*, also known as *hyperlinks*, on a web page and move forward and backwards between web pages.

- To *bookmark* web pages for revisiting at a later time.

Launching Google Chrome

To launch Google Chrome, tap its icon on the Home or All Apps screen or on the Favorites tray, shown below.

The **Welcome to Google Chrome** screen opens, as shown below. Tap **Take a tour** to view several pages of notes to help you get started.

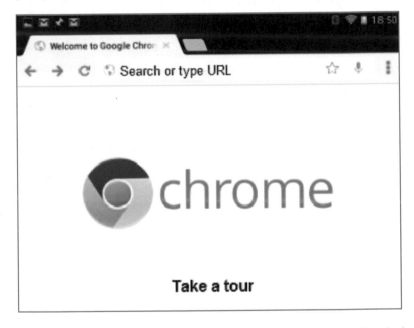

The search bar across the top of the screen is the place to start your web browsing activities. Here you enter either the address of a website or *keywords* which should pinpoint the subject you are interested in.

Entering the Address of a Web Site

Every website has a unique address, known as its *URL*, or *Uniform Resource Locator*. A typical web address is:

www.babanibooks.com

Type the URL into the search bar, as shown below and tap the Go key, shown on the right.

For a complicated address you may need to enter the URL in full. However, in practice you don't often need to be too pedantic; simply entering **babanibooks**, for example, will lead you to the required website. If you've visited a site before, it may appear in a list of suggested sites which pops up to save you typing time.

After entering the address of the website and tapping the Go key on the on-screen keyboard shown on the right above, the site's Home Page opens on the screen, as shown in the extract below.

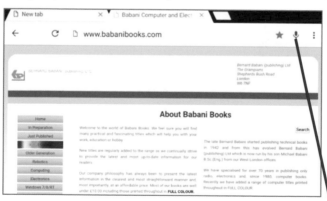

The Voice Search

Instead of typing the URL, as discussed above, tap the microphone icon shown on the right, then speak the web address.

The Keyword Search

This is used to find out about a particular subject rather than visiting a website whose address you know, as discussed on the previous page. The World Wide Web seems to contain pages on every conceivable subject. For example, suppose you wanted to find out about the Border Reivers, who were a major part of the turbulent past in the borders between England and Scotland. Simply enter **border reivers** into the Google Chrome search bar, as shown below. (There's no need to use capital letters when entering search criteria — **Border Reivers** and **border reivers** produce the same results).

After tapping the Go key on the on-screen keyboard, the screen displays a list of Google search results, as shown in the small sample below.

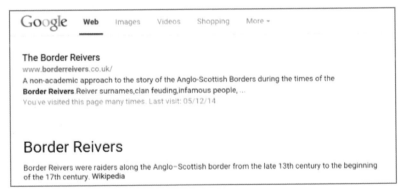

A search often yields millions of results although many may be irrelevant. For example, historians studying the Border Reivers may not be interested in the website of the Border Reivers Rambling Club which might appear in the results. Google puts the most relevant results near the top of the list.

Each of the blue headings on a search result represents a *link* to a web page containing the keywords, **Border Reivers** in this example. Tap a link to have a look at the website.

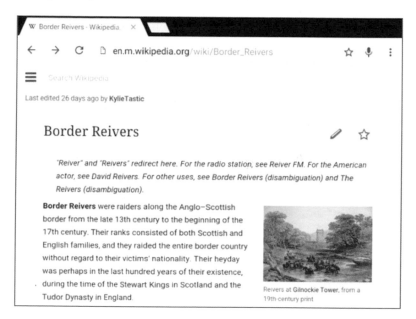

Surfing the Net

On the web page shown above, some words are highlighted in blue. These are *links* which can be tapped to open further web pages. Each new page will probably have lots of further links, so tapping these will open a succession of web pages.

Try typing a few diverse keywords into Google Chrome and see how easy it is to find good information on virtually any subject, no matter how bizarre. Here's a few to get you started:

william shakespeare	cap ferrat	hybrid computer
ssd	quantitative easing	concorde
brunel	peregrine falcon	grace darling

The Internet is surely the world's largest and most up-to-date encyclopaedia covering almost every known subject. At a more practical level, Google Chrome is probably the DIY enthusiast's best friend. Type any DIY task, such as **mending a puncture**, for example, and numerous websites offer helpful advice, often including step-by-step videos.

Previously Visited Pages

The back and forward buttons shown on the right and below allow you to quickly move between recently visited pages. Tapping the circular arrow **Refresh** button on the right and below loads the latest version of a web page. (For speed, the Chrome browser may initially load an earlier web page which is then replaced).

As you move forward or back between web pages, the keywords from each search, such as **shearing a sheep**, are displayed on a tab at the top left of the screen, as shown above and below.

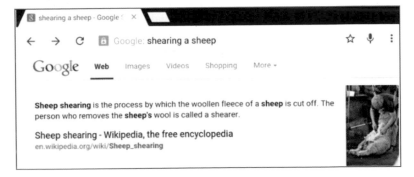

Tabbed Browsing

When you do a search in Google Chrome and then proceed to surf the web, as described earlier, there is only one tab displaying the current web page, as described at the bottom of the previous page. However, Chrome allows you to open each web page in a tab of its own, so that all the tabs are visible along the top of the screen, as shown in the example below.

This makes it easy to move straight to a particular web page, rather than moving through them all one at a time using the back and forward buttons. Tap a tab to open that web page. With a large number of web pages open, the tabs are stacked on top of each other and can be moved around by sliding or gently swiping left or right.

Opening a Web Page in Its Own New Tab

Tap the **New tab** icon shown on the right and below.

A **New tab** appears, as shown above on the right, with the search bar ready for you to enter your search criteria by typing or speaking. After carrying out the search and selecting a web page from the results, this page appears on its own tab. The search criteria, in this case **green woodpecker**, appear on the top of the tab, as shown below, replacing the words **New tab**.

Using the Google Search App

In the previous examples, Google Chrome was opened by tapping its icon on the Favorites tray. You can also launch Chrome after tapping the Google icon shown on the right, on the All Apps screen. Then enter the search criteria, such as **honey buzzard sightings** in this example, in the Google search bar, as shown below.

Google

Tap on a link in the search results to open a web page you want to look at. The web page opens in Google Chrome, in a new tab of its own, **Honey Buzzard**, in this example, as shown below.

To switch to another web page from a previous search, simply tap its tab, such as **mending a puncture**, partly shown above.

Closing a Tab

Close a tab by tapping the cross, as shown below.

Bookmarking a Web Page

You can create a series of *bookmarks* so that you can quickly return to your favourite web pages at any time in the future. With the required web page open on the screen, tap the star shaped bookmark icon as shown on the right and on the right of the search bar below.

The **Add Bookmark** window opens, allowing you to name the bookmark or accept the name suggested by Chrome. Tap **Save** to add the web page to the **Mobile Bookmarks** page. To view the bookmarks, tap the 3-dot menu icon shown on the right and then tap **Bookmarks** on the drop-down menu.

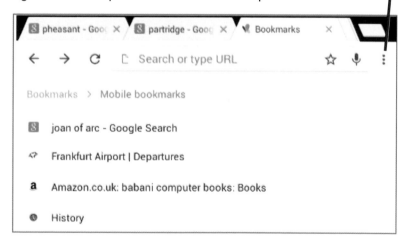

To open one of the bookmarked web pages, tap its icon on the **Bookmarks** page, as shown above. Press and hold a bookmark icon to display the menu shown on the right, including options to edit and delete a bookmark.

| Open in new tab |
| Open in Incognito tab |
| Edit bookmark |
| Delete bookmark |

Displaying Your Browsing History

Google Chrome keeps a record, in chronological order, of all the web pages you've recently visited. Surprisingly there isn't a button to display the History feature. However it can easily be displayed by typing **chrome://history** into the search bar.

When you tap the Go key on the on-screen keyboard, as shown on the right, your **History** list is displayed, as shown below.

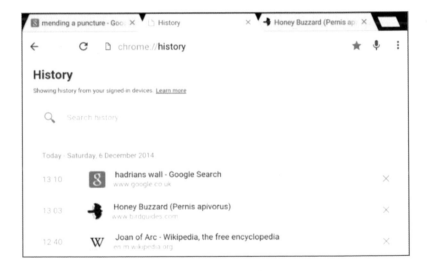

To save time when opening your History list, instead of entering **Chrome://history** into the search bar, create a **History** bookmark, as shown on the right and on page 89. Creating a bookmark is described on page 89. There are options on the History page to **CLEAR BROWSING DATA...** and **Search history**.

Communication and Social Networking

Introduction

This chapter describes the various ways a Lollipop smartphone or tablet can be used to communicate with other people. Some of the main apps used for these activities are:

Gmail

Google e-mail used by businesses, friends and families to send messages, documents and photos all over the world.

Skype

Free worldwide *voice* and *video* calls between computers.

Facebook

The most popular *social networking* website. Enter your personal *profile* and *timeline* and make *online friends* with people having similar backgrounds and interests.

Twitter

Another very popular social networking site, based on short text messages (*140 characters maximum*) which can be read by anyone who chooses to follow the originator, who may be a celebrity, company or a member of the public.

Hangouts

This is Google's own social networking app, which can be used for live video calls, SMS and MMS messaging, group chats and the exchange of photos and videos.

Electronic Mail

Gmail is used for creating, sending and receiving text messages over the Internet. *Replies* can easily be sent to the original sender of a message you've received and to all other recipients of the message. An e-mail can also be *forwarded* to someone else.

Gmail

You can maintain an *address book* for all your contacts and *import* into it files of contacts from other e-mail services.

An e-mail message can include photos and documents, known as *attachments,* "clipped" to the message and sent with it.

Gmail is a web-based e-mail service, so you can access your electronic correspondence from anywhere in the world. All you need is a connection to the Internet and your Gmail username and password, as discussed on page 25.

The Gmail icon in Lollipop shown above gives access to Gmail **and any other e-mail services you use**. After tapping the Gmail icon, tap the 3-bar menu button and select the e-mail account you wish to use, as shown on the right.

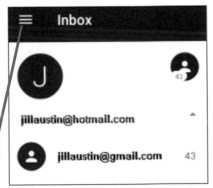

Creating a Message

Tap the 3-bar menu button at the top left of the screen, shown above, then tap the **Compose** icon at the bottom right of the screen, shown here on the right. The **Compose** screen opens, as shown on the next page. Enter the main recipient's e-mail address in the **To** bar. Tapping the small arrow on the far right of **To** opens two new lines for recipients who will receive either Carbon copies (**Cc**) or Blind carbon copies (**Bcc**). The latter don't know who else has received a copy of the message.

Receiving an E-mail

The recipient can read the e-mail in their *Inbox*. They will see the sender's name and the text and photos as shown above.

To open an attached document, tap its name or the paperclip icon, as shown on the right. Tap the star icon on the right to mark the e-mail as a *favourite*. Icons at the bottom of the message, as shown below, allow you to reply to the sender, reply to all recipients of the message or forward the e-mail to someone else.

Skype

This app allows you to make *voice* and *video* calls all over the world. Calls over the Internet are free. If you use a tablet to dial a phone number there is a charge, for which you need credit in a Skype account. You can also send photographs and instant text messages or make and send a video.

The Skype app in the Google Play Store is free and, if necessary, can be installed as described in Chapter 3.

Start Skype by tapping its icon on the All Apps screen, as shown on the right. Then sign in using an existing Skype username and password or a Microsoft account, or create a new Skype account. When you sign in, contacts from your address book are displayed, as shown below.

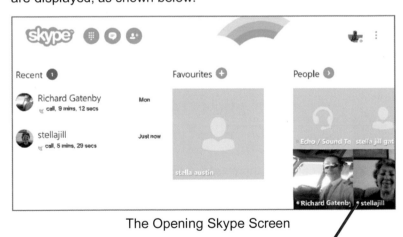

The Opening Skype Screen

Making a Skype Call

Any contacts currently online are displayed with a green dot, as shown on the right and above.

Tap the name or thumbnail of a contact who is currently online.

The following icons are available when making a Skype call:

Start a voice only call   Start a video call

When you call a contact, their photo and name appear on your screen. The functions of the icons are listed below.

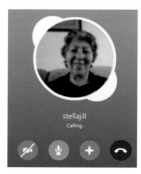   

Making a Skype call   Receiving a call

Receiving a Skype Call

When someone "Skypes" you, the smartphone or tablet will emit a distinctive ring and the caller's name appears on the screen as shown above on the right. Tap the green phone icon shown on the right above to answer the call.

The Main Skype Icons

     Answer a video or voice call

     Switch video on or off

     Switch microphone on or off

    Show dialling pad and messages

    End or reject a call

Hangouts

This is Google's own social network and is similar to Skype, just described. It can be used on all of the main platforms, such as Android, Apple iOS and PC via Google Chrome. You need to have a Google Account and if necessary install the **Hangouts** icon shown on the right from the Play Store, as discussed in Chapter 3.

Hangouts allows you to make voice and video calls. You can invite up to 9 other people to join online conversations and to share photos and videos. You can also send and receive SMS and MMS text messages. The *Hangouts Dialler* app shown above on the right allows you to make calls to a phone number from a tablet. Charges may apply.

Invite Jean to Hangouts

CANCEL   INVITE

Having selected a name or names from your contacts tap either of the icons shown on the right and below to make a video or voice call.

The Hangouts call procedure, shown on the right, is very similar to that just described for Skype.

Messenger

This is a separate, more basic app for sending and receiving SMS and MMS text messages.

Facebook

Facebook is the biggest social network, with over a billion users all over the world. To join Facebook, you must be aged over 13 years and have a valid e-mail address. You can access Facebook using the Android Facebook app, if necessary installed from the

Facebook

Play Store, as discussed in Chapter 3. You also need to *sign up* for a Facebook account and in future *sign in* with your e-mail address and password.

First you create your own *Profile* in the form of a *Timeline*, as shown below. This can include personal details such as your schools, employers and hobbies and interests. Facebook then provides lists of people with similar interests, who you may want to invite to be Facebook *friends*. Anyone who accepts will be able to exchange news, information, photos and videos with you.

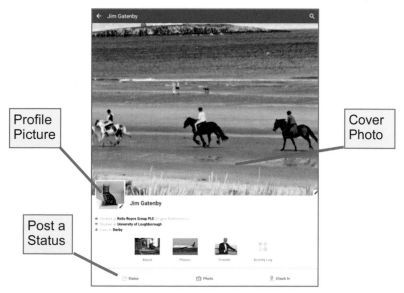

A Profile Picture or Cover Photo can be changed after tapping anywhere within the image.

Security and Privacy

The *audience selector* shown on the right appears against the items of personal information in your profile. Tapping the audience selector displays a drop-down menu, as shown on the right, enabling you to set the level of privacy for each item, ranging from **Public** to **Only me**. **Public** means *everyone* can see the information, including people you don't know.

Status Updates

These are used to post your latest information and news and usually consist of a short text message and perhaps one or more photos. Tap **Status** on the bottom left of the Facebook screen, shown on the previous page, to open the **Write Post** window shown below. Tap **To:** to select the audience. Then enter the text of your post, replacing **What's on your mind?** shown below.

Tap the camera icon at the bottom left of the screen to insert a photo from the internal storage of the tablet.

Finally tap **Post**, shown on the right above and your friends will receive the update in their *News Feed*.

Twitter

Like Facebook, Twitter is a social networking website used by hundreds of millions of people. There is a free app for Twitter in the Google Play Store. If necessary, the app can be installed as discussed in Chapter 3. Signing up to Twitter is free. Once signed up you can either use your e-mail address and password to sign in or you can enter your Twitter username such as **@jimsmith**. Some of the main features of Twitter are:

Twitter

- Twitter is a website used for posting text messages, known as *tweets*, of up to 140 characters in length.
- You can include a 160 character *personal profile* on your Twitter page.
- Photographs can be posted with a tweet.
- Twitter is based on people *following*, i.e. reading the tweets of other people, such as celebrities, politicians and companies marketing their products or services.
- You can follow anyone you like, but you can't choose who follows you. If you have no followers, anything you post on Twitter will remain unread. You could encourage your friends and family to follow you and each other on Twitter, to share your latest news.
- *Hashtags*, such as *#climatechange*, for example, make it simple for other people to find all the tweets on a particular subject. The hashtag is included within a tweet. Tapping the hashtag displays all the tweets on that subject, which might be a campaign or a debate.
- If you like a tweet, it can be *retweeted* to all of your followers, together with comments of your own.
- You can send *replies* to a tweet.

Sending a Tweet

Tap **What's happening?** at the bottom left of the Twitter Home screen and then start typing your message, as shown below.

The number **64** at the top right above is the number of letters still available to be used, out of the maximum of 140 allowed.

Two icons appear at the bottom of the **Tweet** window, as shown below. Tapping the left-hand icon uses the GPS system in your tablet or smartphone to pin-point your current location and include this as a note in the Tweet.

Inserting a Photo into a Tweet

Tapping the right-hand icon above displays the two icons shown here on the right. The camera icon is used to take photos with either of the device's built-in cameras. The right-hand icon is  used to browse for and select a photo already saved on the device. The picture is then included in the tweet, as shown above When the tweet is finished, tap the TWEET button, as shown at the top of this page. Your followers will see your tweet on their Twitter Home screen, as shown on the next page.

Responding to a Tweet

If the reader taps a tweet, the following toolbar is displayed.

These icons enable you to respond to a tweet in various ways. Reading from left to right, they are:

Reply, **Retweet**, mark as **Favorite** and **Share** with other people

Switching on the Display of Photos in a Tweet

To ensure that photos are displayed in a tweet, as shown above, tap the 3-dot menu button at the top right of the screen, shown here on the right, then tap **Settings** and **General**. Tap to place a tick in the box next to **Image previews** to display photos in a tweet. If the box is not ticked, a blue text link is displayed instead, as discussed on the next page

Viewing Photographs in a Tweet

As discussed on the previous page, depending on the **Settings**, instead of a photo, the reader of a tweet may see a blue link embedded in the text, such as **pic.twitter.com/N6taV3lmv3** shown below. This link is created by Twitter automatically .

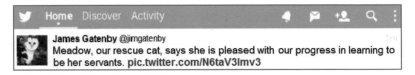

Tap the blue link to display only the photo, enlarged to fill the screen. Tap anywhere on the ordinary text of the tweet to display the entire tweet with the photo enlarged, as shown below.

Photos and the Clouds

Introduction

Smartphones and tablets which use the Lollipop operating system are an ideal platform for taking and managing photos and videos. Most of these devices have a front facing camera for taking "selfies" and making video calls with Skype or Google Hangouts, as discussed in Chapter 8. A higher resolution rear camera is usually provided for general photography.

Cloud storage systems such as Google Drive and Dropbox have simplified the sharing of photos and other files and accessing them from any device, such as a tablet, smartphone or other type of computer anywhere in the world. As discussed in the last chapter, the use of e-mail and social networking sites like Facebook and Twitter have also made it easy to share photos with other people.

The following topics are discussed in this chapter:

- Taking a photo (or making a video) with one of the two cameras built into a Lollipop smartphone or camera.
- Importing photos onto the device from an SD card, micro SD card or flash drive.
- Using Bluetooth wireless technology to copy photos and other files between devices.
- Using a laptop or desktop PC to copy and manage files.
- Sharing or *syncing* photos between devices using cloud storage systems such as *Google Drive* and *Dropbox*.
- Printing to any printer using Google Cloud Print.

Using the Built-in Cameras

Tap the camera icon shown on the right, on the All Apps screen, Home screen or Favorites tray. This will launch the rear camera ready for you to take an ordinary photograph. To make a video call, when using Skype for example, the front camera launches automatically showing your face.

Switching Between Front and Rear Cameras

Tap the **Camera** icon shown above then tap the 3-dot circular menu button shown on the right. Next tap one of the two icons shown on the right below to switch between front and rear cameras. The icon changes as shown, depending on which camera is currently selected.

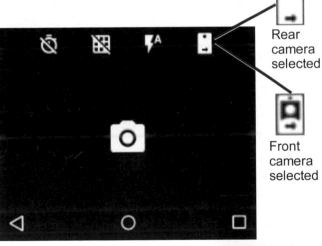

Rear camera selected

Front camera selected

Selecting Photo or Video Mode

Swipe in from the left and tap either **Camera** or **Video** from the menu on the left of the screen, shown here on the right.

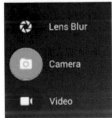

Taking a Photo

Select **Camera** as shown on the previous page at the bottom right. Then tap the black and white **Camera** icon, shown here on the right, to take a photo with the selected camera. You will hear a noise as the photo is taken.

Making a Video

Select **Video** as shown on the previous page at the bottom right. Then tap the video camera icon shown on the right to start recording. Tap the square in a circle icon shown on the right to end the recording.

Viewing Photos and Videos

Thumbnails of photos taken with the smartphone or tablet can now be viewed after tapping the **Photos** icon, shown on the right, on the All Apps screen.

Tap to open a photo, then tap the 3-dot menu button shown on the right. This displays options including **Details**, **Print** and **Slideshow**.

Capturing a Screenshot

To capture a copy of the screen, simultaneously hold down the **Power** button and the **Volume** button (at the volume *down* end). The screenshot can then be viewed in the **Photos** app as described above, or sent using the sharing button shown below on the right. Shown on the right is a screenshot, as used in this book, of the All Apps screen on a Nexus 9 tablet.

The *sharing* button shown on the right often appears and can be used to send a photo to Dropbox, Google Drive, e-mail, Facebook and Twitter, etc., etc.

Some Useful Accessories

Various accessories, as shown below, can be connected to your smartphone or tablet to enable the importing of photos and other files from external sources.

OTG Cable

This connects the Micro USB port on an Android device to a full-size USB female port, allowing various USB devices such as an SD card reader, flash drive and digital camera to be connected.

The OTG cable

USB Flash Drive

Also known as a *memory stick*, this can be connected to the OTG cable for the transfer of files such as photos to an Android tablet or smartphone, perhaps from a laptop or desktop PC.

USB flash drive

USB Battery Charger Cable

The battery charger cable supplied with your smartphone or tablet can be used to connect the Android device to a laptop or desktop PC, using the OTG USB cable shown above. The PC can then be used to manage the transfer of photos and other files to and from the smartphone or tablet.

USB Card Reader

These can take SD cards from a digital camera, for importing photos to a smartphone or tablet.

USB SD card reader

Micro SD Adaptor

Some Android devices have a slot for a Micro SD card. Using an adaptor as shown on the right, the Micro SD card can be used in an ordinary digital camera. Then the photos can be transferred to your smartphone or tablet via the Micro SD slot. The adaptor also fits into the SD card slot in many laptop or

Micro SD adaptor and card

desktop PCs and printers. This enables the transfer of photos and other files between PC and Android devices.

HDMI Cable

This connects the Micro HDMI port fitted to some Android devices to an HDMI monitor, projector or TV, so that photos, videos, etc., on the Android can be viewed on a large screen.

Chromecast

The **Chromecast** is a thumb-sized *dongle* which plugs into a port on an HDMI television. Then videos, web pages, photos etc., on the tablet or smartphone can be viewed on a TV screen.

Chromecast

The input source on the TV should be set to HDMI.

Install the Chromecast app from the Play store, as discussed in Chapter 3. Then open the required photo or video, etc. The Cast button appears at the top right of the Lollipop screen or smart phone, as shown on the right and below. Tap the Cast button to mirror the Lollipop screen to the big screen.

Chromecast

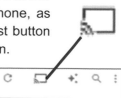

A Cast button also appears on Quick Settings shown on page 56.

Using the Micro USB Port

The *Micro USB* port built into the Android tablets and smartphones and shown on page 18 can easily be converted to a full-size standard USB port using an OTG (On The Go) cable, as shown on page 106.

The OTG cable can be used for connecting USB devices (as indicated below) to the Android device for the importing of files.

- A standard SD card in a USB card reader.
- A USB flash drive/memory stick.
- A separate digital camera.

Importing Photos from a USB Device

The Nexus Media Importer app is free and can be downloaded and installed from the Play Store as discussed in Chapter 3. Connect the USB device to the smartphone or tablet using the OTG cable. The USB device is detected and in response to **Choose an app for the USB device**, tap **Nexus Media Importer**. Then tap **OK**, as shown below, to allow the Nexus Media Importer to access the USB device.

1. Nexus Media Importer
Homesoft
★ ★ ★ ★ ✦

Nexus Media Importer

Allow the app Nexus Media Importer to access the USB device?

☐ Use by default for this USB device

CANCEL   OK

Tap **All Photos** or **Folders** to open thumbnails of the photos on the device, as shown at the top of the next page.

Viewing Photos Stored on an SD Card, etc.

To view a large version of a photo on the SD card or flash drive, double tap a thumbnail, as shown above. You may wish to keep your photo collection on separate SD cards and always view them from the storage medium in this way.

Copying Photos to the Internal Storage

If you wish to save copies of photos on the internal storage of the tablet or smartphone, tap a thumbnail to display the tool icons shown below and on the top right above.

 Saves a **Copy** of the photo on the internal storage of the Android device in the **Pictures** folder, discussed shortly.

 The **Move** button saves a photo in the **Pictures** folder on the internal storage and deletes the original image from the SD card, or flash drive, etc.

 The **Delete** button removes photos from a USB storage medium such as an SD card or flash drive, etc.

 Use the **Share** button to send copies of photos to e-mail, **Photos**, Facebook, Twitter, Dropbox, Google Drive, etc.

 This **Menu** button has options including **Edit**, **Slide Show** and **Rotate,** etc.

Images sent to the **Photos** app, etc., using **Share** above are stored in the "clouds" as discussed in more detail shortly.

Copying Photos Using Bluetooth

In this example a photo is copied wirelessly from a Blackberry smartphone to a Nexus 9 tablet. The same general method can be used to copy between two Android devices using Bluetooth.

Pairing the Nexus 9 with the Blackberry

- In **Settings** on both devices, make sure Bluetooth is **On** and each device is set as **Discoverable** or **Visible to all Bluetooth devices nearby**.

- The phone should be detected and listed on the Nexus 9 under **Available devices**. Tap the name of the phone.

- Confirm that the same **PIN** number appears on both the Nexus 9 and the phone (a Blackberry in this example).

- The two devices are now *paired*, as shown below.

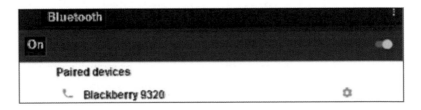

- Open the required photo full-size on the Blackberry.

- From the phone menu, select **Send** then **Bluetooth**.

- On the phone select **Nexus 9** under **Select Device.**

- The file transfer starts.

- On the Nexus 9, swipe down from the top to open the **Notifications** and tap **Do you want to receive this file?** and then tap **Accept** under **Accept the file?**

- The photo can then be viewed on the Nexus 9. Tap the **Photos** icon, then tap the 3-bar menu and select **On device**, as discussed at the top of page 111.

Copying a photo using NFC is discussed on page 65.

Viewing Photos on the Internal Storage

As stated on the previous page, you can save photos in the **Pictures** folder in the internal storage of a smart phone or tablet. To view the photos tap the **Photos** icon on the Home or All Apps screen as shown on the right.

Then tap the 3-bar menu icon on the top left of the **Photos** screen, as shown on the right.

From the drop-down menu which appears, tap **On device** to open the screen shown below.

The thumbnails can be enlarged by double tapping. You can also display options to **Edit**, **Share** and **Delete** photos after single tapping the thumbnail.

Managing a Lollipop Device Using a PC

Connect the Android to a USB port on a PC using the Android's battery charger cable. For example, when I connected my Nexus 9 to a laptop PC using a USB cable, the Nexus 9 **Pictures** folder appears in the Windows Explorer as shown below.

You can then use the PC to manage the photos and other files on the Android tablet or smartphone by dragging and dropping or copying and pasting, deleting and renaming, etc.

Google+ Auto-Backup

The Auto-Backup feature saves copies of your photos to the clouds, including those you take with the internal cameras on the tablet or phone and those you download from other sources.

To check that **Auto-Backup** is **On**, tap the **Photos** icon, then tap the 3-dot menu button. Next tap **Settings** then **Auto-Backup**. If necessary, tap the button to switch **Auto-backup On**, indicated by a blue button as shown below on the right.

Images listed in **On device** in **Photos**, discussed on page 111, may not be backed up automatically but this facility can be switched on using the cloud icon shown below on the right.

Against any group of photos in **On device** such as **Pictures** shown below, there is a cloud icon. If the cloud has a line through it, tap the icon. The cloud changes to blue, as shown on the right, indicating that **Auto-Backup** is **On** for the **Pictures** folder.

With the blue cloud indicating that auto-backup is **On**, all the photos you import will be backed up to the clouds. The new photos will now appear in **Photos** as well as **Photos/On device**.

To see the backed up photos type **#autobackup** in the **Photos** search bar, as shown below.

Managing and Editing Photos

Open the **Photos** app as described on the previous page and then tap the image you wish to manage. Tap the 3-dot button on the top right of the screen to open a menu which includes options to **Print**, **Copy to album** or display in a **Slideshow**.

On the lower right of the screen is an *auto enhance* icon, shown here on the right. Along the bottom of the **Photos** screen shown on the right is a toolbar, shown again below.

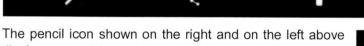

The pencil icon shown on the right and on the left above displays an editing toolbar, with tools to auto enhance, crop, rotate and fine tune the image.

The dustbin icon shown on the right and on the upper toolbar above is used to delete the selected photo.

The sharing icon shown on the right allows you to send a copy of a photo to numerous destinations, shown on the right below, such as Dropbox, Google Drive, Facebook, Twitter, etc., etc., and to include a photo in an e-mail message.

As discussed over the page, Google Drive and Dropbox are cloud storage systems.

Dropbox   **Drive**

Using the Clouds

Introduction

Cloud computing is the *uploading* and storage of *files* such as photos and documents on Internet computers known as *servers*, managed by companies such as Google.

Files stored in the clouds can be accessed by any computer with an Internet connection. Two of the most popular cloud storage systems are Google Drive and Dropbox. With a photo open in Dropbox or Google you can use the **Share** icon shown on the right to send a *link* to the photo to various destinations or to include the link in an e-mail to a friend.

Google Drive

Google offers 15GB of free storage for Drive, Gmail and Google+ Photos and more for schools and business. You can also buy extra storage. The app for Google Drive can be downloaded free from the Play Store, as discussed in Chapter 3. You also need to have set up a Google Drive e-mail address and password.

On any other computers which you use, install the app or, on laptop and desktop PCs, install a **Google Drive** *folder*, after visiting the website at **www.drive.google.com**. Next tap **Install Drive for your computer**. Repeat this for all the computers

Drive

you wish to automatically sync files to. Photos can be uploaded to Google Drive using the Share icon as discussed on page 113.

Google Docs

This is a suite of office apps which is part of Google Drive. It's accessed by tapping the **Drive** icon shown above, followed by the **New** icon shown below.

 New document

Google Docs includes fully-featured word processing and spreadsheet apps as shown below.

Documents are easily saved in the clouds and can then be accessed by any computer, after signing in to Google Drive.

Dropbox

This provides up to 2GB of free storage space while more is available for a monthly fee. If necessary the Dropbox app can be downloaded from the Play Store and you then sign up with your e-mail address and password. As with Google Drive, the Dropbox app should be installed on all of the Lollipop devices you want to sync files to. A Dropbox *folder* must be installed on any PC machines after logging on to **www.dropbox.com**. Photos are uploaded to Dropbox using the Share icon as discussed on page 113.

Google Drive and Dropbox on Windows PCs

Once you've installed Google Drive and Dropbox on PC machines running Microsoft Windows, **Dropbox** and **Google Drive** folders appear in the Navigation pane on the left of the Windows screen, as shown here on the right. Files can be dragged from their location on the hard drive on the PC and dropped into the **Dropbox** or **Drive**  folder. Then they will be synced to all your machines and available on your tablet or smartphone using the Dropbox or Google Drive app.

Cloud Printing Using Lollipop

Google Cloud Print is a free app used for printing from a tablet or smartphone and installed from the Play Store as described in Chapter 3.

If you have a printer connected by a cable to a laptop or desktop PC, this is referred to as a *Classic* printer and needs to be set up in the Google Chrome Web browser as described below. (A *Cloud Ready* wireless printer connects to the Web without being attached to a computer. This shouldn't need any setting up).

For setting up, a classic printer is attached to a laptop or desktop computer which has Chrome installed. Open Chrome on the PC and make sure you're signed in with your Gmail address and password. Open the Chrome menu by clicking the icon shown on the right.

From the menu, select **Settings** and then scroll down the screen and at the bottom select **Show advanced settings**. Scroll down the next screen and under **Google Cloud Print** select **Manage** and then **Add printers**. Select the printer you wish to use, as shown below. Then tap **Add printer** to complete the process.

Google cloud print _beta_

Printers to register

Google Cloud Print has detected the following printers connected to your computer. Click below to add the selected printers to Google Cloud Print for account jimgatenby59@gmail.com.

This step is not required to print to Google Cloud Print. Clicking "Add printer(s)" will just add your local printers to your account. Cloud Ready Printers can connect directly without this step.

✓   EPSON XP-312 313 315 Series

To print an image in **Photos**, open the photo full size and tap the 3-dot menu button and tap **Print**. Select your printer after tapping in the top left-hand corner of the screen and finally tap the Cloud Print icon shown on the upper right. To print a document in Google Docs, tap the middle icon shown on the right, then tap the **Print** icon, which appears as shown here on the bottom right.

Index